Sous Vide Cookbook

The Essential Sous Vide Cookbook for your Every Day Sous Vide Meals - With Over 120+ recipes

Savannah Doss

Copyright Legal Information

Table of Contents

5

Introduction

Sous vide simply means 'under vacuum' in French, but it will come to mean a great deal more to you. It gives you total control over your cooking by taking the guesswork out of cooking times, temperature control, and the answer to your furrowed brow that is asking 'is it cooked?'

Not only will you be sure your food is cooked, you will be delighted to find that it is cooked very well.

Sous vide cookers operate by heating a water bath to a specific temperature, and sustaining that heat in order to cook your food evenly, all the way through. Unlike conventional methods, when you cook with a sous vide cooker, your food is kept in a sealed container. This ensures that all the flavor and moisture is retained as your food gets cooked to perfection. The outer layers of your meat will no longer suffer at the hands of overheated grills as you wait for the middle to cook through. Gone are the days of wilted, over-steamed vegetables! Sous vide recipes are adapted to ensure every ingredient gets the love and care it deserves - inside and out. And so do you! Because everything is sealed in sous vide cooking, you and your family won't miss out on any of the nutrients ordinarily lost in traditional cooking methods.

By following the recipes in this book, you will discover a new appreciation for cooking with the added benefits of using a precision cooker. For skilled cooks who have done it all before, the new methodology will bring greater depth to your skill set. For those who see the kitchen as something of a mystery, these recipes expect only the smallest bit of intuition, and the control you gain over your cooking will rival even the most experienced chef.

While we would like to thank you for purchasing this book, we also hope that you receive a great many more thanks from the very fortunate people who get to enjoy the meals you create.

What is Sous Vide Cooking?

Sous vide cooking involves cooking food by submerging it in a water bath. This is done at a low temperature over a longer period of time than you would ordinarily be accustomed to. The basis of this method lies in the understanding of the food you eat at a molecular level. Happily, the hard work in this regard has been done for you. The result is a cooking method that has been developed thanks to the findings of hundreds of years of food science.

The different foods we eat, at a cellular level, are all unique. If they were all the same, they would essentially be the same food. If you've got certain members of the family who argue that potatoes are sufficient for their vegetable intake, this might be a dream come true for you. As with many things in life, however, it isn't that easy. Each different type of food consists of different proteins which in turn have different characteristics. Among them, the point at which they denature -- recognizable in cooking as going from raw, to cooked.

Sous vide recipes take into account the difference between the proteins that make up the ingredients they are working with. A 'hot pan' or 'medium heat' can mean a great many things and are used in and even broader range of recipes. The research that has gone into sous vide means that the writer can confidently say 55°C for 40 minutes, knowing that at this temperature and for this time, the protein in question will cook just right. If a cooking method were a suit for your ingredient, sous vide would be tailored to perfection.

Additionally, the lower temperatures mean that other elements besides the proteins in your food are broken down differently. Meat proteins are held together by tissues containing collagen, which, if cooked slowly, is hydrolyzed to form gelatin. Having gelatin in your meat provides greater succulence, and the lower temperature means that this is achieved without having to heat the proteins in the meat to the extent that they toughen. Vegetables are often made to wilt due to the breakdown of the stabilizing cell wall common to plant cells. Due to the reduced temperature of sous-vide cooking, the sugars that bind the vegetable cells together are broken down without compromising this structure, effectively separating the cells without breaking them down completely.

It should come as no surprise then, that the method was adopted in restaurant kitchens before machines suited to home cooking were introduced. With its scientific level of precision, chefs running busy kitchens could take the risk out of cooking produce that might otherwise need to be thrown away as a result of under- or over-cooking. The additional benefit comes from the vacuum-seal (the 'vide') of the bag. The natural flavors are not lost while the food cooks -- they simply have nowhere to escape to.

Essential Kitchen Equipment

Sous Vide Machine

You have two different options for sous vide cooking at home - an integrated all-in-one machine, or an immersion circulator. Both will produce excellent results, and the choice of one over another is mostly down to personal preference.

All-in-one Machines

The all-in-one machine is larger, roughly the size of a home kitchen deep fryer. Because everything is integrated, using one is a matter of turning the machine on and getting started.

Immersion Circulator

These are the more portable, smaller option when it comes to sous vide cooking. About the length of a hand blender, they can be stored in cupboards or large drawers when not in use. Using them involves clipping them on to your water container so that the heating element is submerged. They maintain a constant water temperature by then circulating the water they heat, removing any hot or cold spots in your water.

Water Containers

If you have an immersion circulator, you will need a container to use it with. While just about anything capable of holding water heated to a high temperature will work as a water container, these are not all equal in reliability. Crucially, whether or not you are able to cover your container to stop evaporation will have an effect on your final result. Water balls (see below) are one way of achieving this coverage.

Most sous vide users will recommend a polycarbonate container designed for sous vide cooking. These are light, and have the added advantage of being produced with lids that take into account the size and shape of many of the immersion circulators on the market.

Bags

While the sous vide machine provides the constant temperature, the vacuum is achieved through the use of bags which have all remaining air removed before submerging them in the water.

Ziplock Bags

These bags are easy to find online and in-store and come in a variety of sizes. While there are bags designed especially for sous-vide cooking, ziplock freezer bags will work perfectly fine in temperatures below 70°C (158°F). The most important thing to be mindful of when using these bags is that they are freezer quality - these have a more durable sealing mechanism than non-freezer bags.

Sous Vide Bags

If in doubt, choose the bag that is purpose-built! sous vide bags can be found online and don't require a vacuum-sealer as air will naturally seep out of the bag as it is submerged.

Vacuum-sealer

While great results can be achieved without a vacuum-sealer, these are a great way of keeping your ingredients fresher for longer in the lead up to cooking, and ensuring any butterfinger moments don't result in a bag full of water. With lighter ingredients like vegetables, an absence of air will stop the bag from floating in the water too much.

Canning Jars

Heating plastic for prolonged periods of time is something that many cooks will be uncertain about. While the types of plastic used in sous vide and ziplock bags are food safe and used extensively amongst sous vide cooks, many will prefer to stick to glass. Canning jars are needed if you prefer to cook this way, however they are not suited to every type of recipe. Before cooking sous vide with canning jars, make sure you have found a tested recipe to support it.

Water Balls

Water balls, similar to ping pong balls, are designed to sit on the water as it heats up and while your food cooks. The benefits of this are threefold:

- Water stays warmer for longer, reducing the overall energy consumption of your sous vide machine
- Evaporation is minimized by limiting the surface area of exposed water, removing the need to top up and therefore alter the water temperature
- The need for a specialized water container that comes with its own lid is removed, letting you use something you already have on hand

Frying Pan

The low temperatures used in sous vide cooking mean that the browning you ordinarily achieve from searing meat and fish does not occur during cooking time. For this reason you will need a pan on which to quickly brown your ingredients, giving them an appetizing color and outer texture. The pan needs to be very hot in order to minimize time searing and therefore the risk of overcooking.

Ideally you will have a heavy non-stick pan on which to complete this final step so as not to risk having your beautifully cooked meal come apart moments before you serve it just because it got stuck to the pan!

Blowtorch

If pan work is still too high-risk for you, blow torches are a great way of getting the charring on the outside of your meat after it has come out of the machine.

Sous Vide Rack

A rack that sits at the bottom of your water container and serves to separate your food pouches if you are cooking more than one. These are an especially efficient way of keeping pouches from touching, which will lead to uneven cooking as the water can no longer get to all surfaces of your meat or vegetables.

Tips & Tricks for Sous Vide Cooking

As with any cooking technique, sous vide comes with its own set of tricks to minimize the difficulty of producing the best results. This is by no means an exhaustive list but it will get you started on your mission to becoming a sous vide master.

Oil your bag

Often the food you're cooking will seem lubricated enough when uncooked - especially meat and fish - but during the heating process and with the bag being so tightly wound around the ingredients, things can still get a bit stuck. Putting a little bit of oil in your bag will address this problem, especially where things have snuck into the corners.

Weigh the bag down

When food is light or there are some unavoidable air pockets in your bags, you'll find that they float and therefore some of your food is not completely submerged. By putting something heavy - think an old butter knife or spare change - into its own bag, then either putting it in with your ingredients, or attaching it to the outside, you will be able to keep everything under water.

Dry your meat prior to searing

Meat that is still wet (a natural result of sous vide cooking) will not brown as well as dry meat. Using paper towels, remove moisture before putting your meat onto a hot pan (or blowtorching!).

No vacuum? No problem!

Submerging the bag you are using in water once the ingredients are inside has a natural vacuum effect. Use your other hand to squeeze out any extra air bubbles and ziplock, or clip the bag to the container so no water can enter.

Seal your meat and fish in bulk

Vacuum-sealing restricts oxygen from getting to your produce, thereby slowing the activity of any bacteria which can cause food to spoil. If you do have a vacuum-sealer, sealing cuts in advance of cooking them will keep them fresher for longer, and make cooking them as simple as taking them out of the fridge and putting them into your machine. Using this method, however, is no safe-guard against contamination, so always use discretion and keep note of when your meat was purchased.

Blanch before bagging

Blanching any product before putting it into a bag will help to kill any bacteria on the surface. For vegetables, this can reduce browning during cooking. Meat and fish will hold their shape better during the bagging process as the blanching will firm them up.

Salt after cooking

Traditional methods always dictate that you salt your meat before you cook it. On a hot pan, this is certainly the best way to season. However, given the low temperature of sous vide cooking, salting your meat before cooking can initiate a curing process and cause the outside texture to toughen. Salt your meat after you remove it from its bag, before searing.

Sous Vide Basics

Turning on your sous vide machine

A recipe will tell you how hot you need your water bath to be for perfect results. If you have an integrated sous vide water oven, it's as simple as turning it on and setting the temperature. If you are using an immersion circulator, you will need to clip this onto the side of your water container (see Essential Kitchen Equipment) so that submerged as per the device's instructions. From here you need to set the water temperature you require, and wait while for the water to heat.

Preparing your food

Oil the bag you are using to cook your sous vide meal in. Place all necessary ingredients inside and vacuum-seal the bag. This can be done either by submerging the bag almost to the top in a container of (cold) water - either in the sink, a large pot, or your sous vide machine prior to the water getting too warm. Seal your bag if it has a zip lock. If you are using a bag with no zip lock, you will be able to achieve a vacuum environment by submerging it in the water until the food is totally covered, then clipping the bag to the side of the machine.

If you have a vacuum-sealer, once the ingredients are all in the bag, all you need to do is seal it as per your machine's instructions, and the bag is ready to go.

Putting your food into your sous vide machine

Once your water is the right temperature, place your sealed bags in, or if they are unsealed, clip them onto the side of the machine so that the food is submerged but the opening will not let any water in. Set a timer as per the recipe and leave the produce to cook, checking back every now and then to make sure that all parts are submerged. If cooking more than one bag at a time, no two bags should touch in a way that will cause parts of the meat or vegetables to be under-exposed to the surrounding environment.

What can I cook?

The adaptability of the sous vide machine means that it's really more a matter of what you can't cook. The main thing that needs to be taken into consideration is the texture of the food itself. sous vide cooking has a lot of the benefits of slow-cooking, and the prime targets are the foods that have longer cooking times which you often struggle to achieve a consistent texture with. This means larger red meat cuts, pork, hard vegetables and firmer fish.

Eggs are a common hero of sous vide cooking as well - gone are the days of runny whites and hard yolks, the precision method means that timing and temperature have been tested to provide consistently wonderful results.

What can't I cook?

Foods that generally have a fast cooking time benefit more from traditional methods. Exposure to a low temperature for a long time will often result in dulled leaves (think Asian greens, spinach etc.) or a tougher consistency (thin cuts of very tender meat).

Any food that is intended to have a dry exterior (battered or breaded foods) will not get the exposure to air that is required to create this texture. Moreover, the outside will become soggy and unpalatable as it sits in the bag, soaking up the juices of the food it is coating.

Sous Vide Frequently Asked Questions (FAQ)

Is sous vide cooking safe?

Keeping food at temperatures above refrigeration, without reaching the high temperatures traditionally used for cooking can be concerning at first. As with the preparation of any meat or fish, making sure that the cut is fresh is the best first step to ensuring safe consumption. Keeping meat at temperatures between 5°C (41°F) and 60°C (140°F) for more than four hours is widely regarded as unsafe. This applies to the center of the meat especially - even if you are cooking for this long at a temperature above this range, it does not guarantee that the center will reach a safe temperature within the 4-hour period. Recipes will take this into account, but if you are ever cooking a larger cut without a specific recipe, it is important to keep this in mind.

How much can I cook at a time?

This is largely dependent on the size of your water container. If you have a sous vide rack (see Essential Kitchen Equipment), you can keep multiple bags separated while in the container. The key to consistent results is not overfilling the cooking space as you risk pouches touching and therefore their contents cooking unevenly. So, as long as you can maintain this separation, the world is your oyster!

How important is the power of my sous vide machine?

While all machines on the market are designed to produce consistent results, a higher-powered machine will have certain advantages. While it's true that you heat your water to a certain temperature and the machine maintains this, the addition of your pouches may bring the temperature down again. This is because they are unlikely to be as warm as your water when they go in, and a heat transfer from the water to the pouches happens to address this imbalance. A more powerful machine will be able to bring the water temperature up again more rapidly.

Can I season foods the way I like?

Absolutely! What's more, the seasoning needn't be added in as great a quantity as it usually would. This is because of the time spent infusing with the ingredients they are complementing. Try using half the amount of herbs or spices as a starting point.

Salt, however, should be added after removal from the pouch, before you brown your food. See 'Tips and Tricks for sous vide Cooking.'

Can I cook different ingredients at the same time?

Given the very precise nature of sous vide recipes, temperature and timing is tailored to the ingredient being cooked, in order to achieve the best flavor and texture. Vegetables require higher temperatures than meat, so either your meat will be overdone, or your vegetables underdone, losing you the main advantage of sous vide precision.

Can I save sous vide leftovers?

You can save your leftovers the same way as you would other cooked foods. Generally it is safest to consume these within 48 hours of cooking.

Can I cook my meat from frozen?

You can put frozen food directly into your sous vide machine, as water bathing is a highly efficient defrosting method. Extending your cook time by 15-30 minutes depending on the thickness of your cut will thaw it out before starting the cooking process. Check on your food in this time to check for the point at which it is completely thawed, and begin timing its cooking once it has reached this stage.

Breakfast

Navigating the kitchen in the morning is tricky enough without having to grapple with the logistics of pots, pans, and slippery poached eggs all at once. The results can often be underwhelming, and the effort excessive.

It's no secret that sous vide machines are an egg's best friend, and with the stress taken out of your morning meals, they might become yours too

Sunday Special Scramble

Serves 2

Ingredients

2 oz. breakfast sausages, crumbled	1 tablespoons butter
1/4 cup Mexican cheese, grated	Salt to taste
4 large eggs, well beaten	Pepper powder to taste

Instructions

1. Follow the operating instructions and fill the sous vide cooker with water.

2. Preheat the sous vide cooker to 167°F.

3. Heat a pan over a medium flame. Add the sausages and cook until they are browned.

4. Line a medium bowl with paper towels and shift the cooked sausages from the pan into it. Once cooled, keep the sausages in a ziplock bag or a vacuum-sealed bag. Add the eggs, butter, cheese, salt and pepper and vacuum-seal the ingredients.

5. Immerse the bag and cook in the sous vide cooker for 15 minutes. Take out the pouch in between and mix well and immerse it again. Cook until the eggs get the consistency you desire.

6. Remove from the sous vide cooker and serve hot.

Cheesy Eggs with Brioche

Serves 2

Ingredients

3 large eggs

3 brioche buns

2 scallions, green parts only, thinly sliced

1/2 cup Parmesan cheese, grated

1/4 cup cheddar cheese, grated

Freshly ground black pepper powder to taste

Salt to taste

Instructions

1. Set your sous vide machine to 149°F.

2. Keep the eggs on a slotted spoon and gently lower the eggs in the water bath and cook in the cooker for 45 minutes.

3. While that is done, make wells in the brioche buns by pulling out the bread, big enough so the egg can fit in.

4. Gently crack an egg each into the buns. Garnish with cheddar and Parmesan cheese.

5. Place on a line-baking sheet and broil in an oven until the cheese melts.

Canadian Bacon

Serves 4

Ingredients

8 slices Canadian bacon or ham

1 teaspoon vegetable or canola oil

Instructions

1. Set your sous vide machine to 145°F.

2. Place ham into a ziplock or vacuum-seal bag. Remove as much air as you can from bag by using the water displacement method or a vacuum-sealer.

3. Place into the hot water bath and cook for at least 6 hours or up to 12 hours. Cooked ham can be seared and served immediately, refrigerated for up to 1 week, or frozen for up to several months.

4. To serve, preheat a skillet with a tablespoon of oil over medium-high heat. When hot, sear the ham until crisp and browned.

Spiced Oatmeal with Compote

Serves 1

Ingredients

For the oatmeal

1 cups quick cooking rolled oats

3 cups water

⅛ teaspoon ground cinnamon

A pinch salt

For the fruit compote

¾ cups mixed dried fruit of your choice

like raisins, blueberries etc.

⅙ cup white sugar

Zest of an orange, finely grated

Zest of a lemon, finely grated

½ cup water

Instructions

1. Set your sous vide machine to 155°F.

2. Place all the ingredients for the oatmeal into a ziplock or vacuum-seal bag. Remove the air by using the water displacement method or a vacuum-sealer.

3. Repeat with the fruit compote ingredients.

4. Submerge both the bags in to the water bath and cook for 6 to 10 hours.

5. When ready, remove the bags. Shake the oatmeal bag to evenly distribute the oats and then transfer into serving bowls.

6. Serve with the fruit compote.

Easter Ham & Eggs Scramble

Serves 2

Ingredients

8 spears of asparagus, trimmed, cut diagonally into ½ inch pieces

½ sweet onion, peeled, chopped into small pieces

½ red bell pepper, deseeded, chopped into small pieces

8 eggs beaten

2 tablespoons butter

2 oz. heavy cream

4 oz. cooked ham, chopped into small pieces

Pepper to taste

Salt to taste

1 teaspoons herbes de Provence

Instructions

1. Set your sous vide machine to 167°F.

2. Place a skillet over medium high heat. Add butter and melt. Add asparagus, bell pepper and onions and sauté until tender.

3. Transfer into a ziplock or vacuum-seal bag and then add the rest of the ingredients.Remove the air by using the water displacement method or a vacuum-sealer.

4. Submerge in the water bath and cook for about 15-18 minutes. Remove the bag a couple times during the cooking process to shake the contents; submerge again to continue cooking. Cook until the eggs are of the consistency you desire.

5. Remove from the water bath and serve.

Garlic Mushrooms on Toast

Serves 4

Ingredients

10 oz. white mushrooms, sliced 1/2 inch thick

4 tablespoons butter, melted

2 cloves of garlic, crushed

4 large slices of your favourite bread

Grated Parmesan cheese and chopped parsley, to serve

Instructions

1. Set your sous vide machine to 185°F.

2. Place the mushrooms, butter, and garlic in a ziplock bag, ensuring they are well-combined. Remove the air by using the water displacement method or a vacuum-sealer.

3. Place the bag in your sous vide cooker for 1 hour.

4. 5 minutes before your mushrooms are ready, put your bread in the toaster.

5. Remove mushrooms from the cooker and serve on toast with parmesan and parsley.

Perfectly Poached Eggs

Serves 4

Ingredients

6 large eggs

Instructions

1. Set your sous vide machine to 167°F.

2. Place the whole eggs into a ziplock or vacuum-seal bag. Remove the air by using the water displacement method or a vacuum-sealer.

3. Let the eggs cook for 15 minutes.

4. Remove and serve.

Spiced Apple Porridge

Serves 2

Ingredients

4 oz. rolled oats

⅔ cup milk

1 cup water

1 apple, diced into ½ inch pieces

1 teaspoon cinnamon

½ teaspoon nutmeg

Honey or maple syrup to serve

Instructions

1. Set your sous vide machine to 140°F.

2. Mix oats, milk, water, apple, cinnamon, and nutmeg in a large bowl until everything is well combined.

3. Place the mixture into two 10 oz. canning jars and place these in your water bath, making sure they are not secured too tightly.

4. Cook for 10 hours. Make sure your machine has a lid, or you are using sous vide balls to minimise evaporation.

5. Serve in bowls or eat straight from the jar, drizzling with honey or maple syrup to taste.

Smoked Salmon & Asparagus Egg Muffins

Serves 6

Ingredients

6 eggs

¼ cup crème fraiche

¼ cup cream cheese

4 spears asparagus

2 oz. smoked salmon

2 oz. chèvre

½ oz. minced shallot

2 teaspoons chopped fresh dill

Salt & Pepper to taste

Six 4 oz. canning jars with metal lids

Instructions

1. Set your sous vide machine to 170°F.

2. In a blender, mix the eggs, crème fraiche, cream cheese, and salt. Set aside.

3. Chop asparagus into small pieces and add it into a small mixing bowl.

4. Chop smoked salmon into small pieces and add to the bowl with the asparagus. Add minced shallot and dill. Stir until all the ingredients are evenly mixed through.

5. Divide the asparagus and salmon mixture evenly between the six jars. Pour the egg mixture into each jar. Top each jar with a piece of chèvre and attach lids. Make sure lids are loose enough to allow air pressure to be released while cooking.

6. When ready, remove the jars from the bath and serve. Leftovers can be stored in the refrigerator for up to 4 days and reheated in a toaster oven or broiler.

Caramelized Leek & Salmon Egg Muffins

Serves 6

Ingredients

6 eggs

1/2 cup unsweetened almond milk

2 medium leeks, thinly-sliced

1 tablespoon olive oil

Pinch of salt

4 oz. cooked salmon

Six 4 oz. canning jars with metal lids

Instructions

1. Set your sous vide machine to 170°F.

2. In a blender, mix the eggs and almond milk until smooth. Set aside

3. Heat up the olive oil in a skillet over medium high heat. Add the leeks and a pinch of salt. Reduce the heat to medium and sauté until leeks soften and start to caramelize. Make sure to keep stirring to prevent burning. When leeks are golden brown, remove from heat and set aside.

4. In a small bowl, combine the salmon and leeks. Stir until evenly mixed.

5. Spoon the leek mixture between the 6 jars and pour the egg mixture on top.

6. Attach the lids, keeping it loose enough to allow the air pressure to release while cooking.

7. Place in the bath and set the timer for 1 hour.

8. When ready, remove from the bath and enjoy. Leftovers can be stored in the

refrigerator for up to 4 days and reheated in a toaster oven or broiler.

Creamy Scrambled Eggs

Serves 4

Ingredients

8 large eggs

4 tablespoons heavy cream

4 tablespoons 2% milk

2 tablespoons butter

A pinch salt

½ cup medium cheddar cheese, grated

Instructions

1. Set your sous vide machine to 170°F.

2. Crack your eggs into a medium sized mixing bowl. Add your heavy cream, milk, and a pinch of salt and whisk. Grate in the cheddar cheese and continue to whisk until all ingredients are well combined.

3. Pour the egg mixture into a ziplock or vacuum-seal bag. Remove as much air as possible by using the water displacement method, or a vacuum-sealer. If using the vacuum-sealer, drop the bag over a counter edge to prevent the sealer from sucking up the egg mixture.

4. Submerge the bag in the water bath to cook for 20 minutes.

5. When ready, remove the bag and lay it flat on a flat surface. Gently massage the egg mixture with oven mitts to distribute the remaining heat and ensure even cooking. After 20 minutes, remove the bag and lay flat on a smooth surface and massage the egg mixture to help ensure even cooking.

6. Place the bag back in the water and cook for an additional 20 minutes.

7. Tip contents into a serving dish and top with some fresh chives or green onions.

Pizza Omelet

Serves 1

Ingredients

3 large eggs, beaten

1 tablespoon whole milk

2 tablespoons extra virgin olive oil

¼ onion, finely chopped

½ tomato, finely chopped

Salt and freshly ground black pepper

2 tablespoons grated aged cheddar cheese

Chopped fresh scallions

Instructions

1. Set your sous vide machine to 167°F and preheat your oven to 390°F.

2. Combine the eggs and milk in a medium ziplock or vacuum-seal bag. Seal the bag using the water displacement technique and then place the bag in the water bath. Set the timer for 10 minutes. Massage the bag every few minutes to ensure even cooking. You can use a glove if needed.

3. Meanwhile, heat 1 tablespoon olive oil in a medium skillet over medium-high heat. Add onion and sauté until they become tender and begin to caramelize. Add the tomato and continue to cook until softened. Remove ingredients from the heat and season to taste with salt and pepper.

4. When the eggs are ready, remove from the water bath and pour the eggs onto a baking sheet lined with parchment paper. Shape

into a round and season with salt and pepper.

5. Top the egg round with the onion and tomato mixture and sprinkle cheese on top.

6. Bake until cheese is bubbly. Garnish with scallions and serve.

Quiche Pots

Serves 4

Extra equipment: Fry-pan, large bowl & four 4 oz. Mason jars

Ingredients

1 tablespoon olive oil

1 tablespoon butter

1 red onion, thinly sliced

6 eggs

1 teaspoon salt

1 teaspoon cracked black pepper

2½ oz. chèvre, crumbled

Butter for greasing

4 sprigs fresh parsley, finely chopped

Instructions

1. Set your sous vide machine to 172°F.

2. Heat olive oil and butter in a fry-pan over a medium heat. Once butter starts bubbling slightly, add the onions. Stir every few minutes. Onions are done when they are completely soft.

4. Grease 4 4 oz. mason jars with butter

3. Whisk the eggs in a large bowl. Add the salt and pepper and distribute among four 4 oz. Mason jars.

4. Distribute the onion and chèvre among the mason jars. Seal lightly and place in the water bath for 1 hour.

5. Remove the jars from the water and serve, garnishing with parsley.

Smoked Salmon on Toast with Sous Vide Egg Yolk

Serves 3

Ingredients

6 large egg yolks

6 slices crisp toasted bread

Crème fraiche or cream cheese, optional

Sliced smoked salmon

1 teaspoon drained capers

1 teaspoon chopped fresh chives

Salt and freshly ground black pepper

Lemon wedges, for serving

Instructions

1. Set your sous vide machine to 143°F.

2. Place each egg yolk into an individual plastic ziplock bag. Carefully remove the air from the bag by using the water displacement method and then seal – do not break the yolk.

3. Submerge the egg yolks into the water bath and clip the bag to the side of the pot. Set a timer for 1 hour.

4. Before the egg is ready, prepare the toast by spreading crème fraiche or cheese over the toast. Fold the smoked salmon slices and layer it on top of the toast.

5. When the egg yolk is ready, remove the bags from the water bath and then gently remove the egg yolk from the bag. Place on top of the toast and sprinkle some capers and chives on top. Season with salt and pepper and serve with a lemon wedge.

Blueberry Muffins

Serves 10

Ingredients

3 tablespoons (45 grams) unsalted butter, melted

3 tablespoons (45 grams) granulated sugar

1 large egg

1 cup (237 mL) whole milk

1 3/4 cups (210 grams) all-purpose flour

1 tablespoon (15 grams) baking powder

3/4 teaspoon (3.75 grams) salt

1 cup (170 grams) fresh blueberries

Instructions

1. Set your sous vide machine to 195°F and then grease 5 glass jars with non-stick oil spray or butter.

2. In a large bowl, whisk together butter and sugar. Whisk in the egg one by one until smooth. Whisk in the milk last.

3. Fold in flour, baking powder, and salt. Mix the batter until just combined, and then fold in the blueberries.

4. Divide the batter evenly between the prepared jars. Fill each jar no more than 2/3 full and then firmly tap the bottom of the jars on the counter to remove air bubbles.

5. Seal the jars until just tight. Do not overtighten to allow space for air pressure to escape.

6. Place the jars in the water bath and cook for 3 hours.

7. When the muffins are ready, remove from the water bath and let it cool on a wire rack. When cool to the touch, remove the lids and then run a knife along the edges to un-mold.

8. Cut each muffin in half and serve.

Cocktails & Drinks

Sous vide cooking isn't just for food! The warm, sealed environment means that you can speed up the process often needed for the infusion of flavors into a drink, such as those of herbs, spices and fruits.

The recipes that follow will guide you through how to develop greater flavors in your mixers, and create flavors that are just a little bit different.

Ponche Crema

Serves 2

Ingredients

4 eggs, beaten well

2 cup water

14 oz. can sweetened condensed milk

12 oz. can evaporated milk

12 oz. can crème de coco

1 ½ cup white rum

3 sticks cinnamon

Powdered cinnamon to garnish

Instructions

1. Fill and preheat the sous vide cooker to 185°F according to the operating instructions.

2. Blend together eggs, water, evaporated milk, condensed milk and crème do coco until smooth.

3. Pour this mixture and cinnamon sticks into a ziplock cooking pouch. vacuum-seal the pouch and submerge in the cooker and cook for 2 hours.

4. Remove the pouch and place in ice water bath for 30 minutes.

5. Strain the liquid and discard the cinnamon sticks and any solids.

6. Place in the refrigerator to chill until use.

7. To serve, pour the chilled mixture into a large bowl. Add rum and stir well.

8. Serve into individual glasses. Sprinkle cinnamon on top.

Christmas Punch

Serves 4

Ingredients

2 cups dried sorrel (hibiscus flowers)

4 tablespoons fresh ginger, minced

1 tablespoon whole allspice berries (Jamaican pepper)

1 cup caster sugar

4 cups water

Instructions

1. Set your sous vide machine to 135°F.

2. Place all the ingredients into a zip lock or a vacuum-seal bag. Fold the edge over a couple times and then clip to the edge of the container or pot. Cook for 30 minutes.

3. Remove and place in an ice water bath for 20 minutes. Strain the solution and pour into a bottle. Discard the solids.

4. Keep chilled in the refrigerator until ready to use. To serve, pour over crushed ice and then garnish with mint leaves.

5. To make a cocktail, add an ounce of rum to a shaker along with the chilled punch. Shake well and then serve with mint leaves as a garnish and a few cranberries.

Christmas Spritzer

Makes approximately 2 cups

Extra equipment: One glass bottle for storage

Ingredients

Zest of 8 oranges	2 cloves
2 cups cognac	Sparkling water
½ cup sugar	Mint, to serve
1 cinnamon stick	

Instructions

1. Set your sous vide machine to 180°F.

2. Put oranges cognac, sugar, cinnamon, and cloves in a ziplock or a vacuum-seal bag. Fold over the top several times and then clip to the edge of the container or pot.

3. Cook for 1 ½ hours.

4. Strain the orange zest from the liquid.

5. Serve 1 part syrup to 2 parts sparkling water, changing the ratio to taste if desired. Garnish with mint.

Store remaining liqueur in the refrigerator for up to one month.

Mr. Figgie Collins

Serves 2

Ingredients

1 dozen semi dried figs, chopped

9 oz. Blanco tequila

2 teaspoons lime juice

1 teaspoon agave syrup

Crushed ice

Soda water to serve

Fig slices to serve

Instructions

1. Set your sous vide machine to 50°F.

2. Place the figs and Blanco tequila in a ziplock or a vacuum-seal bag. Fold over the top several times and then clip to the edge of the container or pot. Cook overnight.

3. Remove the pouch and let it cool naturally. Strain. Discard the solids.

4. Take 100 ml of the infused liquid and place in a shaker. Store the rest in the refrigerator. Add agave syrup and ice and shake

5. Pour in highball glasses over ice. Add soda and garnish with slices of fig.

Herbal Gin & Tonic

Makes 10 oz. of infused gin

Ingredients

10 oz. gin

6 sprigs rosemary

8 - 10 peppercorns

Tonic water

Lemon to garnish

Instructions

1. Set the sous vide machine to 117°F.

2. Place gin, rosemary, and pepper in a ziplock or a vacuum-seal bag. Fold over the top several times and then clip to the edge of the container or pot.

3. Cook for 2 hours.

4. Strain the liquid to remove rosemary and pepper.

5. Serve 1 part gin to 2-3 parts tonic water, serving over ice and garnishing with lemon.

Vintage Pink Lady

Serves 4

Ingredients

To make the infused Pear Shrub

4 oz. Bosc pears, washed, cored, thinly sliced

4 oz. Demerara sugar

4 oz. apple cider vinegar

For the vintage pink lady

3 oz. gin

1 ½ oz. pear shrub

1 oz. fresh lemon juice

½ oz. Demerara simple syrup

4 dashes bitters

2 egg whites

Fresh cranberry juice for garnishing

Ice cubes to serve

Instructions

1. Set your sous vide machine to 148°F.

2. Place the sugar and pears into a ziplock or vacuum-seal pouch. Fold the top over a couple times and then clip to the edge of the pot or container. Cook for 1 hour.

3. Remove and place in an ice water bath for 30 minutes. Remove from the ice bath and then refrigerate for at least 12 hours.

4. The next day, set your sous vide machine to 148 degree. Transfer the sous vide pears into a new ziplock or vacuum-seal bag, and add the apple cider vinegar and mix well. Repeat sealing process and cook for 6 hours.

5. Remove pouch and place in ice water bath for 15 minutes. Refrigerate until chilled.

6. Strain and transfer the liquid into clean glass bottles. Retain the pears for garnish.

7. To make the vintage pink lady, mix together all the ingredients except ice cubes and cranberry juice in a shaker.

8. Shake well and pour into cocktail glasses. Let it sit for about a minute.

Then top with cranberry juice and ice cubes

Mango Lassi

Serves 8

Ingredients

1 quart plus 2 cups whole milk

3 tablespoons yogurt with live active cultures, like full-fat Fage

2 mangos, peeled, pitted, and diced

¼ cup granulated sugar

1 cup ice

1 tablespoon vanilla extract

½ teaspoon kosher salt

Instructions

1. Set your sous vide machine to 115°F.

2. In a medium saucepan over medium heat, heat 1 quart milk to 180°F and then pour the milk into a large canning jar. Let the milk cool until it reaches 100-120°F.

3. Stir the yogurt into the milk and seal the jar with a lid. Place the jar into the hot water bath and set a timer for 24 hours. Cover the water bath with plastic wrap to minimize water evaporation. You may need to add more water to keep the jar fully submerged under water.

4. When the timer goes off, remove the jar from the water bath and transfer to an ice bath. Then refrigerate for at least 8 hours.

5. Combine the remaining 2 cups milk with the mango, ice, sugar, vanilla, salt, and chilled yogurt in a blender. Puree until smooth. Serve immediately.

Spiced Apple Cider

Serves 2

Ingredients

2 bottles apple cider

1 cinnamon stick

1 tablespoon maple syrup

½ teaspoon black peppercorns

2 tablespoons juice from an orange

Instructions

1. Set your sous vide machine to 140°F.

2. Put all the ingredients together in a plastic bag and fold the top of the bag over a couple of times. Clip the edge of the bag to the water bath and cook for 60 minutes.

3. Strain and serve hot.

Mint Julep

Serves 10

Ingredients

2 cups water

2 cups bourbon

1 ½ cups coconut sugar

2 cups fresh mint

Instructions

1. Set your sous vide machine to 135°F.

2. Add the water, bourbon, coconut sugar, and mint to a plastic zip-seal bag and fold over several times to close. Clip the edge of the bag to the bot and cook for 1 ½ hours.

3. Strain and chill. When cold, serve over ice with fresh mint.

Butternut Squash Cordial

Serves 4

Ingredients

4 small butternut squash, peeled, seeded, chopped, juiced

4 cups brown sugar syrup

8 oz. vodka

Instructions

1. Set your sous vide machine to 148°F.

2. Place the strained butternut squash juice and the brown sugar syrup in a ziplock or vacuum-seal bag. Fold the top over a couple times and then clip it to your container or pot. Cook for 45 minutes.

3. Remove and place in ice water bath for 30 minute. Remove from the ice bath and strain through a fine mesh sieve into a glass bottle.

4. In a shaker, add the butternut squash syrup and then the vodka. Shake well to mix and serve over ice. Syrup can be refrigerated for up to 2 weeks.

Vodka Mule Punch

Makes around 3 ½ quarts

Extra equipment: Punch bowl

Ingredients

One 750ml bottle of vodka

2 cinnamon sticks

5 cloves

1 bottle sparkling white wine

1 quart apple juice

1 quart ginger ale

1 bunch mint

Ice cubes

Instructions

1. Set your sous vide machine to 147°F.

2. Put vodka, cinnamon and cloves in a ziplock or a vacuum-seal bag. Fold over the top several times and then clip to the edge of the container or pot.

3. Cook for 2 hours

4. In a punch bowl, mix vodka (leaving or removing spices as desired), sparkling white wine, apple juice and ginger ale.

5. Slap mint to extract flavor and sprinkle into the punch.

6. Serve, adding ice cubes to keep chilled is desired.

Mulled Wine

Ingredients

½ bottle red wine

Juice of 2 oranges, peel of 1

1 cinnamon stick

¼ cup caster sugar

1 bay leaf

1 vanilla pod, sliced in half lengthways

1 star anise

Instructions

1. Set your sous vide machine to 140°F.

2. Combine all of the ingredients in a bowl and stir to mix.

3. Pour the wine into two bags. Fold the top of the bag over a couple of times and then clip it to the edge of your water bath. Cook 1 hour.

4. Serve hot or chilled.

Soups

Soups are often a two step process of getting all ingredients to cook down, then developing flavor. Making soup using the sous vide method brings the advantage of letting your flavors develop as the food cooks, minimising the steps you take in the kitchen, while still treating you and your family and friends to perfectly balanced soups.

Cream of Celery Soup

Serves 2

Ingredients

2 cups celery, diced into large pieces

½ cup russet potatoes, peeled, diced into small pieces

½ cup leek, diced into large pieces

½ cup stock (vegetable or chicken)

½ cup heavy cream

1 tablespoon butter

1 bay leaf

1 teaspoon kosher salt or to taste

White pepper powder to taste

Instructions

1. Set your sous vide machine to 180°F.

2. Place all the ingredients in a ziplock or a vacuum-seal bag. Remove the air by using the water displacement method or a vacuum-sealer. Seal and then submerge in the water bath. Cook for 1 hour or until the vegetables are tender.

3. When done, remove the bay leaf and puree the soup. Strain through a wire mesh strainer and discard the solids. Serve hot.

Carrot & Coriander Soup

Serves 4

Extra equipment: Blender or food processor

Ingredients

1 lb. carrots

1 cup coconut cream

2 teaspoons ground coriander

1 teaspoon ground cumin

1 clove garlic, crushed

Fresh coriander, chopped, to serve

Instructions

1. Set your sous vide machine to 190°F.

2. Put carrots, coconut cream, coriander, cumin, and garlic into a ziplock or vacuum-seal bag and remove all the air with the water displacement method or a vacuum-sealer. Seal and submerge the bag in the water bath and cook for 1 hour and 45 minutes.

3. Transfer the ingredients to a blender, breaking up the carrots as you remove them, and blend until smooth.

4. Serve warm, topping with chopped coriander to taste.

Spring Onion Soup

Serves 2

Ingredients

2 bunches spring onions, rinsed, trimmed, chopped

4 cloves garlic, peeled, chopped

1 large russet potato, peeled, diced

2 teaspoons olive oil plus extra for serving

2 teaspoons soy sauce

Salt to taste

Pepper powder to taste

2-3 tablespoons fresh parsley leaves for garnishing

Instructions

1. Set your sous vide machine to 180°F.

2. Add all the ingredients in to a zip lock or a vacuum-seal bag and remove all the air with the water displacement method or a vacuum-sealer. Seal and submerge the bag in the water bath and cook for 45 minutes to 1 hour.

3. Remove the pouch and transfer into a blender and blend until smooth and creamy.

4. Ladle into individual soup bowls. Garnish with parsley and serve.

Chicken & Vegetable Soup

Serves 2

Ingredients

1/2 cup zucchini, diced

1/2 cup red bell pepper, diced

1/2 cup cauliflower, chopped

3 baby carrots, chopped

1 medium onion, chopped

2 cups fresh spinach leaves

1/2 teaspoon garlic powder or to taste

1/2 teaspoon onion powder

Sea salt to taste

Black pepper powder to taste

Cayenne pepper to taste

1 cup chicken, diced, sous vide cooked

½ tablespoon olive oil

2 cups chicken broth

Instructions

1. Set your sous vide machine to 180°F.

2. Place all the vegetables and spices in a bowl. Mix well and place in to a zip lock or a vacuum-seal bag. Remove all the air with the water displacement method or a vacuum-sealer. Seal and submerge the bag in the water bath and cook for 1 hour or until the vegetables are tender.

3. To make the soup, heat olive oil in a soup pot over medium heat. Add broth and bring to a boil.

4. Lower heat and add chicken and cooked vegetables along with their juices. Simmer for 5-7 minutes.

5. Serve hot.

Cauliflower Soup

Serves 2

Ingredients

1 large head cauliflower, break into florets

2 shallots, chopped

4 cups of vegetable stock

½ cup white wine

½ cup sour cream

1 ½ cups cream

Juice of a lemon

1 teaspoon Ras el Hanout

Zest of 2 lemon, grated

A few slices roasted caraway bread

1 teaspoon ground cumin

Cooking spray

1 cup grated cauliflower to serve

Extra virgin olive oil to serve

Instructions

1. Place a skillet over medium heat. Spray with cooking spray. Add shallot and sauté for a couple of minutes.

2. Set your sous vide machine to 167°F. Place shallots, cauliflower, stock, wine, sour cream, cream and lemon juice into a ziplock or a vacuum-seal bag and remove all the air with the water displacement method or a vacuum-sealer. Seal and submerge the bag in the water bath.

3. Meanwhile mix together grated cauliflower, Ras el Hanout and half of the lemon zest.

4. Remove the pouch from the cooker and transfer into blender and blend until smooth. Season with salt and pepper. Pulse a couple times to mix well.

5. Place the grated cauliflower mixture on bread slices. Drizzle some oil over it. Sprinkle salt, cumin and the remaining lemon zest.

6. Ladle into individual soup bowls. Serve with the garnished bread slices.

Butternut Squash & Apple Soup

Serves 2

Ingredients

1 small butternut squash, peeled, sliced

1 medium apple like Granny Smith, peeled, cored, sliced

3 green onions, trimmed, sliced

1/2 teaspoon sea salt or to taste.

1/2 cup light cream

Instructions

1. Set your sous vide machine to 185°F.

2. Place all the vegetables and apples into a zip lock or a vacuum-seal bag and remove all the air with the water displacement method or a vacuum-sealer. Seal and submerge the bag in the water bath, cook for 2 hours or until the vegetables are cooked through.

3. When done, puree the soup. Add salt and cream and blend again. Serve hot.

Chicken Noodle Soup

Serves 2

Ingredients

3 pounds whole chicken, trussed

3 cups carrots, finely diced

9 cups chicken stock

3 cups white onion, finely diced

3 cups celery, finely diced

Salt to taste

Pepper to taste

2 bay leaves

1 ½ pounds dried egg noodles

Instructions

1. Set your sous vide machine to 150°F.

2. Add all the ingredients except noodles into a large zip lock bag or a vacuum-seal bag. Remove all the air with the water displacement method or a vacuum-sealer. Seal and submerge the bag in the water bath and cook for 6 hours or until the vegetables and chicken are cooked. Cover the cooker with plastic wrap so that the evaporation is kept to the minimum.

3. When done, remove from the cooker. Transfer into a large pot. Place the pot over medium heat.

4. Cook for around 20 minutes. Remove the chicken with a slotted spoon.

5. Add noodles and cook until al dente. Shred the chicken with a pair of forks and add it back into the pot.

6. Heat thoroughly and serve

Borscht

Serves 4

Extra equipment: Large stock pot

Ingredients

2 large beets, peeled and sliced

2 large carrots, peeled and sliced

½ large onion, peeled and sliced

1 small potato, peeled and sliced

¼ head red cabbage, thinly sliced

2 quarts stock of your choice

½ cup chopped fresh dill

3 tablespoons red wine vinegar

Salt and pepper to taste

Sour cream, to serve

Fresh dill, to serve

Instructions

1. Set your sous vide machine to 182°F.

2. Put the beets, carrots, and onions into a ziplock or a vacuum-seal bag and remove all the air with the water displacement method or a vacuum-sealer. Do the same with the cabbage in a separate pouch.

3. Place the bags in the sous vide cooker for at least 1 hour. They can stay in for up to 2.

4. Remove the vegetales. Puree the beets, carrots and onions. Leave the cabbage to the side.

5. Bring the stock to the boil, adding the pureed vegetables, cabbage, dill, vinegar, salt and pepper. Let the soup simmer until you are ready to eat.

6. Serve the soup with a spoonful of sour cream and some fresh dill.

Creamy Tomato Soup

Serves 2

Ingredients

¼ cup butter

3 tablespoons flour

2 ¼ cups milk

½ cup heavy cream

1 ½ cans whole or diced tomatoes, peeled

1 fresh tomato, chopped

1 small green pepper, chopped

1 clove garlic, chopped

1 tablespoon dried basil leaves

A pinch cayenne pepper

Tabasco sauce to taste

½ teaspoon salt or to taste

½ teaspoon black pepper powder or to taste

Instructions

1. Place a saucepan over medium heat. Add half the butter. When the butter starts melting, add flour and sauté for a couple of minutes stirring constantly.

2. Slowly add milk and continue stirring until the mixture thickens.

3. Add cream and continue stirring. Do not boil. Remove from heat and keep aside.

4. Place another saucepan over medium heat. Add the remaining butter. When butter melts, add onions, garlic, and green pepper and sauté until the onions are translucent. Add tomatoes and basil and simmer for a few minutes.

5. Lower heat and add the white sauce, cayenne pepper, Tabasco, salt and pepper.

6. Set your sous vide machine to 172-175°F.

7. Place all the vegetables into a zip lock or a vacuum-seal bag and remove all the air with the water displacement method or a vacuum-sealer. Seal and submerge the bag in the water bath cook for 45 minutes.

8. When done, puree the soup. Serve hot.

Chilled Pea & Cucumber Soup

Serves 4

Extra equipment: Blender or food processor

Ingredients

10 oz. peas

1 onion, diced

1 clove garlic, crushed

2 lebanese cucumbers, seeded, roughly chopped

¼ cup mint leaves

2 cups vegetable stock, chilled

Instructions

1. Set your sous vide machine to 180°F.

2. Put the peas, onion and garlic into a large zip lock or vacuum-seal bag. Seal the bag using the water displacement method or a vacuum-sealer.

3. Cook peas for 1 hour. When done, submerge in an ice bath for 15 minutes.

4. Puree the contents of the bag, with the cucumber and mint.

5. Slowly add the stock until ingredients are well-combined and you reach a smooth consistency.

6. Serve chilled, giving the soup a stir if there is any separation.

Slow Chicken Stock

Serves 12

Ingredients

2 pounds chicken bones

2 cups diced carrots

2 cups diced celery

2 cups diced leeks

2 tablespoons extra virgin olive oil

8 cups water

1 tablespoon whole black peppercorns

2 bay leaves

Instructions

1. Set your sous vide machine to 180°F and preheat your oven to 450°F.

2. In a large bowl, mix together the chicken bones, carrots, celery, and leeks with the olive oil. Place the ingredients onto a sheet pan and roast until golden brown, about 20 minutes.

3. Transfer all of the bones and vegetables, along with any accumulated juices and brown bits on the sheet pan, into a large zip lock or vacuum-seal bag. Add the water, peppercorns, and bay leaves. Seal the bag using the water displacement method or a vacuum-sealer.

4. Submerge the bag in the water bath and set the timer for 12 hours. Cover the water bath with plastic wrap to minimize water evaporation. Continuously top off the pot with more water to keep the bag fully submerged under water.

5. When ready, strain the ingredients and then portion out the stock into airtight containers. Store in the refrigerator for up to 1 week or freeze up to 2 months.

Cornish Hen Stew

Serves 4

Ingredients

2 tablespoons coconut oil

4 medium shallots, smashed and peeled

3 cloves garlic, smashed and peeled

2 lemongrass stalks, roughly chopped

piece fresh ginger, thinly sliced

5 dried red Thai chilies

2 teaspoons dried green peppercorns, coarsely ground

1 teaspoon ground turmeric cups water

2 whole Cornish game hens

1/2 cup chopped cilantro

2 scallions, coarsely chopped

2 tablespoons Asian fish sauce

1 teaspoon finely grated lime zest

Kosher salt and freshly ground black pepper

Instructions

1. Set your sous vide machine to 150°F.

2. In a large skillet, melt the coconut oil over medium heat. When hot, add the shallots, garlic, lemongrass, ginger, chilies, peppercorns, and turmeric. Cook, stirring occasionally, until shallots begin to soften, about 5 minutes.

3. Add the water to the skillet and stir, making sure to scrape the bottom of the pan. Carefully transfer to a large zip lock or vacuum-seal bag. Add the game hens to the bag and then seal using the water displacement method. Place the bag in the water bath and set the timer for 4 hours.

4. When ready, remove the bag from the water bath and take out the hens. Let the hen rest until cool enough to handle. Separate the legs, wings, and breast meat.

5. Add the cooking liquid to a large pot and bring it to a simmer over medium-high heat. Stir in the cilantro, scallions, fish sauce, lime juice, and game hen meat. Season to taste with salt and pepper.

Curried Chicken Soup

Serves 8

Ingredients

1 (4-pound) whole chicken, trussed
6 cups water
2 cups diced carrots
2 cups diced celery
2 cups diced white onion
Kosher salt and freshly ground black pepper
1 tablespoon coconut oil
1 cup thinly sliced shallots
2 tablespoons red curry paste

1 tablespoon curry powder
2 garlic cloves, minced
1 teaspoon ground turmeric
1 teaspoon ground coriander
1 teaspoon sugar
1/2 teaspoon crushed red pepper
4 cups fresh spinach leaves
1/4 cup thinly sliced scallions
1 tablespoon fish sauce
Cilantro and lime wedges, for serving

Instructions

1. Set your sous vide machine to 150°F.

2. In a large zip lock or vacuum-seal bag, combine the chicken, water, carrots, celery, and onion. Season with salt and pepper. Seal the bag by using the water displacement technique or a vacuum-seal. Set a timer for 6 hours. Cover the water bath with plastic wrap to minimize water evaporation. Continuously top up the pot of water to keep the chicken fully submerged.

3. When the timer goes off, remove the bag from the water bath. Remove the chicken from the bag and then strain the soup with a fine mesh strainer. Discard the rest of the vegetables.

4. Let the chicken rest until cool to the touch, then remove and shred the meat.

5. Heat the coconut oil in a stockpot or Dutch oven over medium heat. Add the shallots and cook until softened.

6. Stir in the curry paste, curry powder, garlic, turmeric, coriander, sugar, and crushed red pepper. Continue to cook for 5 minutes, and then add in the reserved chicken cooking liquid and bring to a simmer. Continue to simmer for 30 minutes to allow the flavors to meld.

7. Near the end of the cooking process, add the spinach, scallions, fish sauce, and shredded chicken. Simmer until heated through and the spinach has wilted, about 2 minutes. Season to taste with salt and pepper. Serve topped with cilantro and lime wedges.

Stracciatella Soup

Serves 8

Ingredients

1 (4-pound) whole chicken, trussed

6 cups water

2 cups diced carrots

2 cups diced celery

2 cups diced white onion

Kosher salt and freshly ground black pepper

1/2 cup grated Parmesan cheese

4 large eggs, beaten

1/4 cup thinly sliced scallion

2 tablespoons freshly squeezed lemon juice

2 tablespoons minced fresh parsley

2 cups baby spinach

Instructions

1. Set your sous vide machine to 150°F.

2. In a ziplock or vacuum-seal bag, combine the chicken, water, carrots, celery, and onion. Season with salt and pepper. Seal the bag using the water displacement technique and then place the bag into the hot water bath. Set a timer for 6 hours. Cover the water bath with plastic wrap to minimize water evaporation. Continuously top off the pot with water to keep the chicken fully submerged.

3. When the timer goes off, remove the bag from the water bath and carefully remove the chicken from the bag. Strain the cooking liquid through a fine-mesh strainer into a stockpot. Discard the rest of the ingredients.

4. Let the chicken rest for about 20 minutes or until cool to the touch. Remove and shred the meat.

5. Bring the cooking liquid to a simmer over medium-high heat.

6. In a medium bowl, whisk together the Parmesan, eggs, scallion, lemon juice, and parsley. While stirring the stock, slowly pour in the egg mixture in a thin ribbon. Let the eggs cook undisturbed for 1 minute, and then stir.

7. Add the spinach and shredded chicken and simmer until heated through and the spinach has wilted. Season & serve.

Oyster Stew

Serves 4

Ingredients

4 tablespoons unsalted butter

1 cup thinly sliced leeks

1 small garlic clove, minced

2 cups shucked oysters with liquid

2 cups whole milk

2 cups heavy cream

1 bay leaf

Kosher salt and freshly ground black pepper

Instructions

1. Set your sous vide machine to 120°F.

2. Melt the butter in a large skillet over medium heat and then add the leeks and garlic. Sauté while stirring until the vegetables are tender. Set aside to cool.

3. In a large zip lock or vacuum-seal bag, combine the oysters, milk, cream, bay leaf, and leek mixture. Seal the bag using the water displacement method or a vacuum-sealer and then place in the water bath. Set the timer for 1 hour.

4. When the timer goes off, remove the bag from the water bath. Divide the stew into bowls and remove the bay leaf. Season with salt and pepper to taste and serve.

Salads

Salads might not come to mind when you think about slow cooking, but the salads below might turn the head of even your fussiest eater. With recipes designed to bring out the absolute best in your ingredients, preparing your salad ingredients sous vide might be the difference between finding a new home for the broccoli, and stopping your loved ones for fighting over the last bit!

Fresh Beetroot Salad

Serves 2

Ingredients

½ pound fresh beets, scrubbed, trimmed, halved

2 cups salad greens, torn

For the vinaigrette dressing:

1 tablespoon sherry vinegar

¼ teaspoon salt

1 tablespoon fresh chives, minced

½ tablespoon extra-virgin olive oil

Instructions

1. Set your sous vide machine to 185°F.

2. Place the beets in to a ziplock or a vacuum-seal bag and remove all the air with the water displacement method or a vacuum-sealer Seal and submerge the bag in the water bath and cook for 1 hour or until the beets are tender.

3. When ready, quickly chill the beets in an ice water bath.

4. Peel the beets and dice into bite sized pieces.

5. To make the vinaigrette, whisk together vinegar, salt, and chives. Slowly drizzle in the olive oil and whisk until emulsified.

6. Place the chopped beets in a salad bowl. Pour in the dressing and toss well.

7. Chill in the refrigerator for at least 10 minutes for the flavors to meld.

8. To serve, divide the greens into plates and top with the beets.

Green Sesame Salad

Serves 4

Extra equipment: Small bowl for whisking

Ingredients

2 cups broccoli, snapped into small florets

1 cup green beans, topped and tailed

1 cup asparagus stems, cut in half

2 tablespoons soy sauce

1 teaspoon sesame oil

1 tablespoon vegetable oil

1 teaspoon fish sauce

1 handful sesame seeds

¼ cup scallions, finely chopped

Instructions

1. Set your sous vide machine to 180°F.

2. Place the vegetables in to a ziplock or a vacuum-seal bag and remove all the air with the water displacement method or a vacuum-sealer. Seal and submerge the bag in the water bath and cook for 10 minutes, and up to 20 if you prefer a more tender texture.

3. While vegetables are cooking, whisk together the soy sauce, sesame oil, vegetable oil and fish sauce in a small bowl

4. Put the vegetables into a large bowl and pour the dressing over, using your hands to mix everything through.

5. Sprinkle with sesame seeds and scallions and serve.

Spiced Pear Salad

Serves 2

Ingredients

4 firm pears, peeled, cored, halved

6 pods cardamom, lightly crushed

½ cup maple syrup

2 tablespoon brandy

1 fresh vanilla pod, split and seeds scraped

2 cups walnuts, toasted

2 cups blue cheese, crumbled

For the Dressing

6 tablespoons white wine vinegar

¼ cup extra virgin olive oil

2 tablespoons poaching liquid – refer to step 3

¼ teaspoon salt

¼ teaspoon pepper powder

4 small heads frisee

Instructions

1. Set your sous vide machine to 158°F.

2. Place the pears and cardamom pods in to a zip lock or a vacuum-seal bag and remove all the air with the water displacement method or a vacuum-sealer. Seal and submerge the bag in the water bath and cook for 30-40 minutes or until the pears are tender but still has a bit of hardness.

3. Remove the pears from the pouch and set aside. Retain the poaching liquid.

4. Mix together the ingredients of the dressing. Whisk well until emulsified.

5. Divide the frisee into serving bowls and drizzle the dressing over it. Sprinkle the crumbled cheese over the frisee. Finish off with walnuts and half a pear.

Carrot & Dill Salad

Serves 4

Ingredients

1 lb. thin baby carrots, peeled

2 tablespoons unsalted butter, melted and cooled

¼ cup fresh dill, finely chopped

Sea salt flakes

Instructions

1. Set your sous vide machine to 183°F.

2. Put the carrots and butter into a ziplock or vacuum-seal bag and and remove all the air by using the water displacement method or a vacuum-sealer. Seal the bag.

3. Place the bag in your sous vide cooker for one hour.

4. Put the carrots into a large bowl, adding the dill and tossing with your hands until it is well-combined.

5. Serve warm and add sea salt flakes to taste.

Cocktail Shrimp Salad

Serves 4

Ingredients

20 shrimp or small prawns, shelled and de-veined

2-4 bunches romaine lettuce (depending on if you want a starter or main size), chopped into bite-sized pieces

1 avocado, sliced into bite-sized pieces

2 scallions, chopped

1 cup of cherry tomatoes, halved

Salt and pepper

2 tablespoon mayonnaise

1 tablespoon ketchup

2 teaspoon lemon juice

Extra lemon wedges to serve

Instructions

1. Set your sous vide machine to 149 F.

2. Place your shrimp into a zip lock or vacuum-seal bag and remove all the air by using the water displacement method or a vacuum-sealer. Seal shut and submerge in the water bath for 15 minutes.

3. In a large bowl, combine all of the salad veggies

4. In a small bowl, whisk together the mayonnaise, ketchup, and lemon juice to make the dressing. Season with salt and pepper to taste.

5. When the prawns are done, drain and pat dry with some clean paper towels. Toss the shrimp in the dressing.

6. To serve, portion out the vegetables onto a plate and spoon the dressed shrimp on top. Serve with a lemon wedge and some tabasco on the side.

Warm Broccoli Salad

Serves 4

Ingredients

3 heads broccoli, washed, chopped into florets (or use 6 heads broccoli and omit cauliflower)

3 heads cauliflower, washed, chopped into florets

½ cup extra virgin olive oil, divided

20 cherry tomatoes, quartered

6 anchovy fillets, rinsed, cut into pieces

Salt to taste

Pepper powder to taste

Instructions

1. Fill and preheat the sous vide water bath to 183 degrees F according to the operating instructions.

2. Place the cauliflower and broccoli in a bowl. Sprinkle half the olive oil, salt, and pepper. Toss well.

3. Transfer into a Ziploc bag and vacuum-seal it.

4. Submerge the bag in the water bath and cook for 45 minutes.

5. Meanwhile place the tomatoes in a bowl. Add olives and anchovies and set aside.

6. When the vegetables are cooked, discard any liquid remaining in the pouch and transfer the vegetables into the bowl of anchovies.

7. Sprinkle the remaining olive oil. Add some salt and pepper. Toss well and serve.

Pickled Fennel Salad

Serves 4

Ingredients

1 bulb of fennel, thinly sliced

½ tsp yellow mustard seeds

½ cup white wine vinegar

1 tablespoon fine sugar

2 sweet oranges, sliced into thin wedges

Fennel fronds (if on hand)

Fresh parsley, roughly chopped

Sea salt flakes

Olive oil, to serve

Instructions

1. Set your sous vide machine to 180°F.

2. Dissolve the sugar in the vinegar by heating it gently in a saucepan. Allow to cool.

3. Place the fennel, mustard seeds, and vinegar mixture into a ziplock or vacuum-seal bag. Remove all the air with the water displacement method or a vacuum-sealer.

4. Place into your water bath for 30 minutes.

5. Remove the fennel from the pickling liquid and toss with orange, fennel fronds, and parsley. Drizzle with olive oil, add salt to taste, and serve.

German Potato Salad

Serves 2

Ingredients

¾ pound red or yellow potatoes, cut into chunks of ¾ inch

¼ cup chicken stock

Salt to taste

Pepper powder to taste

2 oz. thick cut bacon, cut into ¼ inch thick slices

¼ cup onions, chopped

2 ½ tablespoons cider vinegar

2 scallions, thinly sliced

Instructions

1. Set your sous vide machine to 185°F.

2. Place the potatoes and chicken stock into a large ziplock bag or a vacuum-seal bag. Remove all the air with the water displacement method or a vacuum-sealer. Seal and submerge the bag in the water bath and cook for 1 hour and 30 minutes or until the vegetables are cooked.

3. Meanwhile, place a nonstick skillet over medium high heat. Add bacon slices and cook on both the sides until crisp. Remove the bacon and keep aside.

4. To the same skillet, add onions and sauté until translucent. Remove the onions and keep aside.

5. When the potatoes are cooked, remove from the water bath and keep aside.

6. To the same skillet, add the browned bacon and onions. Place over medium heat.

7. When heated thoroughly, reduce heat and add vinegar.

8. Remove the potatoes from the pouch and add to the skillet along with the liquid in the pouch.

9. Simmer thoroughly until the liquid thickens.

10. Remove from heat. Add scallions and mix well.

11. Serve warm.

Fresh Chicken Salad

Serves 2

Ingredients

1 pound bone–in, skinned chicken breast halves

1 lemon, sliced

Zest of half a lemon, grated

1 tablespoon lemon juice

1 small red onion, finely chopped

1 stalk celery, finely chopped

2 cloves garlic, minced

2 whole sprigs tarragon

1 tablespoon fresh tarragon leaves, minced

2–3 tablespoons mayonnaise or to taste

½ tablespoon Dijon mustard or to taste

Kosher salt to taste

Pepper powder to taste

2 teaspoons fresh parsley leaves, minced

2 teaspoons fresh chives, minced

Lettuce leaves to serve

Instructions

1. Set your sous vide machine to 150°F.

2. Sprinkle salt and pepper over the chicken breasts. Place the chicken pieces into a large zip lock bag or a vacuum-seal bag. Remove all the air with the water displacement method or a vacuum-sealer. Seal and submerge the bag in the water bath and cook for 1 to 4 hours or until done.

3. When done, remove the bag from the water bath and place on an ice bath to chill.

4. When cool enough to handle, remove the skin and bones from the chicken and discard it. Chop the chicken into bite sized pieces

5. Add zest, lemon juice, mustard, mayonnaise, minced tarragon, parsley,

chives, onions, celery and garlic to a large bowl. Whisk well.

6. Add chicken pieces, salt and pepper. Fold until well combined.

7. Serve over a bed of lettuce leaves

Garden Salad

Serves 2

Ingredients

2 French radishes or red radishes, quartered lengthwise
2 baby patty pan squash, quartered lengthwise
2 baby zucchini, quartered lengthwise
3 sugar snap peas, trimmed of ends and strings removed
2 slices English cucumber, peeled
2 string beans
2 whole red pearl onions, peeled, halved
2 baby golden baby beets, peeled, quartered
2 baby turnips, peeled, sliced in half
½ carrot, peeled, sliced into 3 inch pieces
1 tablespoon kosher salt or to taste
2 tablespoon extra-virgin olive oil

For the salad
Different types of leaves and flowers to garnish
3 fresh mint leaves, finely chopped
2 oz. fresh Chèvre
3 fresh basil leaves, finely chopped
1 tablespoon chives, finely chopped
3 fresh Italian parsley leaves, finely chopped
1 ½ tablespoons olive oil
2 tablespoons pistachio, toasted, ground
½ tablespoon kosher salt
½ bunch baby romaine
½ bunch arugula
½ bunch watercress
Extra olive oil to drizzle
Juice of a lemon

Instructions

1. Set your sous vide machine to 156°F. Place all the vegetables into separate zip lock bags or vacuum-seal bags. Remove all the air with the water displacement method or a vacuum-sealer. Seal and submerge the bag in the water bath and cook until the vegetables are tender. As the vegetables cook, pull the pouch out and place in an ice water bath to chill for 10 minutes.

2. In a medium bowl, mix together the Chèvre, the finely chopped herbs, olive oil, salt, and nuts. To serve arrange on a serving platter, watercress, and

arugula. Layer the vegetables except the carrots over the watercress and arugula.

3. With a peeler slice the carrots and then spread all over the salad. Drizzle with olive oil and lemon juice. Finish with the chèvre mixture and a sprinkle of fresh herbs and flowers.

Entrées

The meals below are made using methods designed to cook the main ingredients to absolute perfection. Serve them as mains, or tweak the quantities to have them as starters. Remember that while some recipes are complete meals, you may want to add your own sides to others.

Some recipes may have extended cooking times or preparation to consider so it's best to read them through before committing to any. Starting on a quiet afternoon will give you the best chance of really settling in to the use of your sous vide cooker, and give you time to address any problems that may come up as you prepare the meals.

Buttery Lobster Tails

Serves 2

Ingredients

2 large lobster tails

2 tablespoons unsalted butter

2 sprigs fresh tarragon

Lemon wedges, for serving

1/4 cup clarified butter, for serving

Instructions

1. Lay tails flat against a cutting board and slide in two bamboo skewers along the length of the tail to prevent the tail from curling when cooking.

2. Bring a large pot of water to a rolling boil and blanche the lobster tails for 1 minute. Remove tails and transfer to ice bath.

3. Shuck lobster tails by squeezing the sides of the shell until you hear a crack. Then pull the shell outwards to expose the meat. Remove tail meat and set aside.

4. Place meat in a heavy-duty zipper-lock bag or a vacuum bag. Add butter and tarragon. Remove the air in the bag by using the water displacement method or a vacuum-sealer.

5. Set temperature to 130-140°F Add meat to the water bath and cook for at least 20 minutes and up to 1 hour, depending on your desired level of doneness.

6. When ready, remove lobster from bag, discard tarragon, and serve immediately with lemon wedges and clarified butter on the side.

SAY NO TO OVER-CROWDING

Given enough space, delicate foods such as prawns cook beautifully in a sous vide bath. But cram a bunch of them into a bag at once and you'll wind up with a lot of mangled, terrible-looking crustaceans. Overcrowding also dramatically impacts the cooking time, resulting in unevenly prepared food — some pieces overcooked, some still nearly raw.

To avoid this, place pieces carefully inside the bags so that they all have equal access to the warm water surrounding them.

Aromatic Sirloin Steak

Serves 2

Ingredients

3 pounds sirloin steak

1 ½ teaspoons garlic powder

1 ½ teaspoons dried thyme

1 ½ teaspoons cumin powder

½ teaspoon pepper powder

½ teaspoon salt or to taste

For the herb butter

1 stick butter, softened

1 ½ tablespoons fresh parsley, minced

1 ½ tablespoons fresh tarragon, minced

1 ½ tablespoons fresh basil, minced

¼ teaspoon black pepper powder

Instructions

1. Set your sous vide machine to 131°F.

2. Add all the ingredients of steak into a large zip lock bag or a vacuum-seal bag. Remove all the air with the water displacement method or a vacuum-sealer. Seal and submerge the bag in the water bath and cook for 3 to 10 hours or until desired doneness.

3. Meanwhile make the herb butter by whisking the all the butter ingredients. Set aside to firm up a little bit in the refrigerator.

4. Remove the bag from water and remove the steaks from the bag. Pat dry with paper towels.

5. Place it on a preheated grill and grill for a couple of minutes on both the sides.

6. Serve steak with a pat of herb butter.

Cheese-Stuffed Burgers

Serves 2

Ingredients

4 oz. Fontina cheese, sliced into 4, each of ¼ inch

4 oz. Gruyere cheese, sliced into 4, each of ¼ inch

1 pound lean ground beef

Salt to taste

Freshly ground pepper to taste

4 onion buns, split

4 leaves lettuce

4 slices tomatoes

4 slices onions

Sauce of your choice for serving

Instructions

1. Set your sous vide machine to 185°F.

2. Divide the beef into 8 equal portions and shape each part into a thin round patty.

3. Place a piece of Fontina and Gruyere each in between 2 patties and seal the edges of the meat.

4. Sprinkle salt and pepper over the patties. Repeat with the remaining patties.

5. Place the potatoes and chicken stock into a large zip lock bag or a vacuum-seal bag. Remove all the air with the water displacement method or a vacuum-sealer. Seal and submerge the bag in the water bath and cook for 1 hour and 30 minutes or until the vegetables are tender.

6. Place each cheese filled patty in individual ziplock pouches. Repeat sealing process and cook for 1 hour.

7. When done, transfer onto a preheated grill and grill on both the sides until slightly charred.

8. To serve, place a burger on top of a bun and top with lettuce, tomato slices, and onions slices.

Sweet Chicken Teriyaki

Serves 2

Ingredients

2 chicken breasts, skinless, boneless,

cleaned, pat dried

2 teaspoons sugar

1 teaspoon salt

4 tablespoons soy sauce

4 tablespoons sake

1 tablespoon ginger juice

Instructions

1. Brush the chicken pieces with ginger juice. Mix together salt and half the sugar in a small bowl. Sprinkle this mixture on both sides of the chicken.

2. Place the chicken pieces into a large zip lock bag or a vacuum-seal bag. Remove all the air with the water displacement method or a vacuum-sealer. Set aside to marinate for at least 3 – 5 hours.

3. Set your sous vide machine to 140°F.

4. Submerge the bag of chicken in to the water bath and cook for 1 ½ hours or until the chicken is done.

5. Remove the bag from the water and remove the chicken piece. Pat dry with paper towels.

6. Pour the cooking liquid into a small saucepan. Add sake, soy sauce and remaining sugar. Place the saucepan over medium heat and simmer until the sauce has reduced to a syrup.

7. Spread half the sauce over the chicken and place the chicken under the broiler until caramelized.

8. Remove from the broiler and drizzle the remaining sauce and serve.

Salmon Burgers with Lemon Aioli

Serves 4

Ingredients

2 pounds salmon, skin and pin bones removed
10 tablespoons kosher salt for brining
2 quarts water for brining
4 tablespoons capers, rinsed, drained
4 scallions, chopped
4 tablespoons Dijon mustard
2 tablespoons mayonnaise
Juice of 2 lemons
Zest of 1 lemon
½ teaspoon salt or to taste
½ teaspoon pepper powder

1 ½ cups dried bread crumbs
Tabasco sauce to taste
4 tablespoon vegetable oil
8 buns to serve, cut horizontally, lightly toasted
Arugula to serve
For the lemon garlic aioli
½ cup mayonnaise
Juice of a lemon
Zest of a lemon
1 teaspoon roasted garlic, minced
2 teaspoons capers, minced

Instructions

1. Set your sous vide machine to 130°F. Place the salmon and salt into a large zip lock bag or a vacuum-seal bag. Remove all the air with the water displacement method or a vacuum-sealer. Seal and submerge the bag in the water bath and cook for about 30 minutes. Remove the bag from the water bath.

2. Chop the most of the salmon into 1/4 inch pieces and place in a large bowl. Set it aside. Place the rest of the salmon into the food processor. Add mustard, mayonnaise, pepper, Tabasco, lemon juice, and zest and pulse until it forms a paste. Transfer into the bowl of salmon.

3. Add scallions, capers, and salt. Taste and adjust the seasonings if necessary.

4. Divide the mixture into 8 equal portions. Shape into patties. Cover the patties loosely with a plastic wrap and freeze for a minimum of 30 minutes.

5. Meanwhile make the lemon garlic aioli by mixing together all the ingredients of the lemon garlic aioli. Set it aside. Heat a nonstick skillet over medium high heat. Add half the oil. When oil is heated, place 3 - 4 the patties and cook until browned on both sides. Add the remaining oil and fry the remaining patties.

6. To serve, spread aioli onto the buns. Place a patty on each bun. Add some

arugula and then top with the other half of the bun

Asian Flank Steak with Beefsteak Tomatoes

Serves 2

Ingredients

6 tablespoons fish sauce

6 tablespoons maple syrup

5 tablespoons mirin

2 teaspoons sesame oil

Salt and pepper, to taste

1 pound flank steak

1 large beefsteak tomato, cut horizontally into thick slices

1 lime

Fresh cilantro leaves, for garnishing

Instructions

1. Set your sous vide machine to 131°F.

2. In a small bowl, whisk together the fish sauce, maple syrup, mirin, sesame oil and black pepper. Pour it into a medium saucepan and simmer over medium high heat. Reduce until sauce is thick and syrupy, set aside to cool. When cooled, reserve half the marinade.

3. Place the flank steak into a zip lock or vacuum-seal bag and pour in the other half of the sauce. Use the water displacement method or a vacuum-sealer to remove as much air from the bag as possible, and then seal shut.

4. Submerge the bag in the water bath and cook for 1 ½ hours.

5. When the steak is almost done, about 30 minutes, season the tomatoes with salt and pepper and then place in a ziplock or vacuum-seal bag. Remove the air and then submerge in the water bath. After 30 minutes, remove the tomato slices from the bag and brush both sides with some reserve marinade and then grill or pan fry the tomato slices on high heat briefly, or until it starts to caramelize.

6. When the steak is ready, remove it from the water bath and the bag and brush some marinade on top. Grill or sear both sides on high heat for some color. Transfer to a cutting board and then let the meat rest for one to two

minutes. When ready, slice the flank steak across the grain.

7. To serve, portion the tomato slices and top with a portion of the flank steak. Garnish with cilantro leaves and a lime wedge on the side.

Sous Vide Steaks

Serves 2

Ingredients

2 steaks of ½ pound each

Kosher salt to taste

Freshly ground black pepper powder to taste

6 sprigs thyme, chopped

2 cloves garlic, sliced

1 shallot, thinly sliced

1 tablespoon canola oil

Instructions

1. Set your sous vide machine to 180°F.

2. Sprinkle salt and pepper over the steaks.

3. Place the steaks, thyme, garlic, and shallot into a large zip lock bag or a vacuum-seal bag. Remove all the air with the water displacement method or a vacuum-sealer. Seal and submerge the bag in the water

bath and cook for 45 minutes to an hour or until the steak is cooked to your desired doneness. Remove and pat dry with kitchen towels.

4. Heat a skillet on medium heat. Add oil. When oil is heated, sear each side until nicely charred.

5. Let the steak rest for a few minutes before serving.

Curried Vegetables With Mint Yogurt

Serves 2

Ingredients

½ cup cauliflower florets

¼ cup carrots, chopped into matchsticks

¼ cup zucchini, chopped into matchsticks

¼ cup green beans, chopped into 2 inch pieces

¼ cup snap peas

2 teaspoons olive oil

1 tablespoon curry powder

½ teaspoon kosher salt or to taste

⅓ cup yogurt

½ tablespoon lime juice

½ teaspoon chili flakes

½ tablespoon chopped mint

Instructions

1. Set your sous vide machine to 165°F.

2. Place the green vegetables into one zip lock or vacuum-seal bag and the rest of the vegetables in to another.

3. Mix together olive oil, curry powder, kosher salt, yogurt, lime juice, chili flakes, and mint. Divide this between both the bags.

Remove all the air with the water displacement method or a vacuum-sealer. Seal and submerge the bag in the water bath and cook until the vegetables are tender. Green vegetables take about 11 minutes and the other vegetables takes about 2 minutes. As the vegetables cook, pull the bags out to prevent over cooking

4. Serve with bread or rice.

Thai Green Curry

Serves 2

Ingredients

2 chicken breasts

1 ½ cups eggplants, chopped into 1 inch pieces

½ cup pea eggplants

10 kaffir lime leaves, torn in half

¼ cup Thai green curry paste

2 cans coconut milk

¼ cup fish sauce

3 tablespoons palm sugar

4 small red chilies, thinly sliced lengthwise

1 cup Thai basil leaves

2 cups boiling water

Instructions

1. Set your sous vide machine to 185°F.

2. Sprinkle salt and pepper over the chicken. Place the chicken and 2 tablespoons coconut milk into a large zip lock bag or a vacuum-seal bag. Remove all the air with the water displacement method or a vacuum-sealer. Seal and submerge the bag in the water bath and cook for 1 hour and 15 minutes.

3. Meanwhile make the curry by placing a pot on medium heat. Add 1 can coconut milk, and green curry paste. Stir to mix.

4. Add eggplants and the remaining coconut milk. Stir and then add the water to the pot. Let the curry simmer for 15-20 minutes. Add fish sauce and pea eggplants and palm sugar.

5. Stir in half the chili strips and Kefir leaves and let the curry simmer for another 10 minutes.

6. Remove from heat and add the basil. Cover and set aside.

7. When the chicken is ready, remove it from the water and the bag and slice it into bite- sized pieces.

8. Place the chicken slices in individual serving bowls. Pour the curry sauce on top.

9. Garnish with the remaining chili strips and serve over steamed rice.

Stuffed Eggplant

Serves 4

Extra equipment: Small saucepan, fry pan, food processor or mortar and pestle and oven

Ingredients

2 eggplants, cut in half lengthways, seasoned with salt and pepper

⅓ cup quinoa

1 teaspoon cumin seeds

2 teaspoons coriander seeds

1 handful almonds

1 handful shelled pistachios

2 teaspoons salt

Olive oil

Yoghurt and pomegranate seeds, to serve

Instructions

1. Set your sous vide machine to 185°F.

2. Place your eggplant halves into a ziplock or vacuum-seal bag, or multiple bags if required. Drizzle some olive oil in the to bag(s) and seal using the water displacement method or a vacuum-sealer.

3. Place the eggplant into your cooker and cook for 1 ½ hours.

4. Meanwhile, cook the quinoa as per the packet instructions.

5. In a dry fry pan, toast the cumin and coriander seeds on a medium heat until they begin to pop. Lower heat immediately. Remove from the heat and use the same pan to toast the almonds until they are slightly browned.

6. In a food processor or mortar and pestle, crush the cumin, coriander, almonds, pistachios and salt together.

7. Stir the nut mixture into the quinoa and add olive oil until the mixture only just begins to hold together.

8. When the eggplant is ready broil for 5 minutes flesh-side down until the skin is charred

9. Turn the eggplant flesh-side up and cut down the flesh lengthways. Spoon

in the quinoa mix and top with yoghurt
and pomegranate seeds to serve

Rosemary & Lemon-Infused Salmon

Serves 4

Ingredients

4 lbs. wild salmon

2 Tablespoons olive oil

1 Tablespoon rosemary, chopped

Zest of one lemon

Juice of one lemon

¼ teaspoon garlic powder

¼ teaspoon black pepper

⅛ teaspoon sea salt

2 cloves garlic, thinly sliced

2 tablespoons capers

Instructions

1. Set your sous vide machine to 115°F.

2. In a small bowl, whisk together the olive oil, rosemary, lemon juice, zest, salt, pepper, and garlic powder.

3. Place the salmon into a zip lock or re- sealable bag and add the olive oil mixture. Release as much air as possible using the water displacement method or a vacuum-sealer.

4. Place the bag in the bath and set the timer for 30 minutes

5. When ready, remove from the bath and pour the contents onto a shallow soup bowl or a plate with a lip to keep the juices.

6. Heat a tablespoon of olive oil in a frying pan over medium-high heat and sauté the garlic until fragrant and crisp. Remove the garlic with the slotted spoon.

7. In the pan, sear the salmon pieces, skin side down, for 3 minutes or until skin is crispy.

8. Remove the salmon from the pan and garnish with the crispy garlic slices and capers.

Creamy Peas

Serves 8

Ingredients

1 lb. frozen or fresh sweet peas

1 cup heavy/single cream

1/4 cup butter

1 tablespoon cornstarch

1/4 teaspoon ground nutmeg

4 cloves

2 bay leaves

Cracked black pepper

Instructions

1. Set your sous vide machine to 185°F.

2. In a small bowl, whisk together the cream, cornstarch, and nutmeg until the cornstarch is completely dissolved.

3. Add all of the ingredients in a ziplock bag. Use the water displacement method or vacuum-sealer to release as much air from the bag as possible.

4. Submerge in the water bath and set the timer for 1 hour. Use a heavy pot lid to weigh down the bag if necessary.

5. When ready, remove from the bath and pour the contents into a serving dish. Stir. Top with some freshly cracked black pepper and serve.

Chicken Schnitzel & Gravy

Serves 2

Ingredients

2 chicken breasts, pounded
Salt and Pepper to taste
2 teaspoons Worcestershire sauce
¼ teaspoon garlic powder
1 cup dry seasoned breadcrumbs
2 eggs, beaten
3 tablespoons butter

2 tablespoons flour
1 ¼ cups chicken stock
1 tablespoon sour cream
½ teaspoon freshly ground black pepper
Chopped parsley for garnish

Instructions

1. Set your sous vide machine to 134°F.

2. Season the chicken steaks with salt and pepper, Worcestershire sauce and garlic powder. Place the chicken steaks into a ziplock or vacuum-seal bag and remove the air by using the water displacement method or a vacuum-sealer.

3. Submerge in the water bath for 45 minutes.

4. About 20 minutes before the steaks are done, prepare the coating. Place the breadcrumbs into a shallow dish and beat the eggs in another.

5. When steaks are done, remove from the water and the bag and then pat dry with paper towels. Coat the steaks first with the egg and then the breadcrumbs. Repeat one more time for a double coat.

6. Preheat the oven to 200°F.

7. In a cast iron skillet, melt 2 tablespoons butter over medium high heat. Cook each steak for about 1-2 minutes on each side or until the coating is golden brown. When done, remove the steaks from the skillet and keep warm in the preheated oven.

8. Using the same cast iron skillet, make the gravy. Add the remaining tablespoon of butter into the skillet and melt. Stir the flour in until there are no lumps. Gradually whisk in the chicken stock until there are no lumps.

9. Bring the gravy to a boil and then reduce the heat slightly. Continue to cook until thickened, about 2-3 minutes.

10. Remove skillet from the heat and stir in sour cream and black pepper until there are no lumps.

11. To serve, transfer the steak on a plate, and generously coat the top with the gravy. Garnish with parsley and serve immediately.

Citrus-Scented Green Beans

Ingredients

1 lb. trimmed green beans	½ teaspoon salt
2 mandarins, zest and juice	2 oz. hazelnuts, toasted and crushed
2 Tablespoons butter	

Instructions

1. Set your sous vide machine to 185°F.

2. Place the green beans, butter, mandarin zest and juice, and salt into a ziplock bag.

3. Using the water displacement method or vacuum-sealer, remove as much air from the bag as possible

4. Place in the bath and set the timer for 1 hour. Weigh down the bag with a smaller, heavy, pot lid if necessary.

5. Remove the beans from the bath and transfer to a serving plate. Sprinkle some more mandarin zest and garnish with the hazelnuts.

Spiced Pork Loin Steaks

Serves 4

Ingredients

1 - 1.5 lbs. pork loin, cut into 4 steaks

1 Tablespoon cocoa powder

1 teaspoon chipotle chili powder

1 teaspoon garlic powder

1 teaspoon ground cumin

½ teaspoon cinnamon

½ teaspoon salt

8 oz. onion, chopped

¾ oz. poblano pepper, chopped finely

2 tablespoons olive oil

1 can pineapple

Instructions

1. Set your sous vide machine to 145°F.

2. Lay the pork steaks onto a clean chopping board to dry. Meanwhile, combine all the dry spices to make a spice mix.

3. Rub the steak with the spice mix until completely coated. Coat each steak or chop completely with the rub

4. Place the steaks or chops in a ziplock bag or vacuum-seal bag and remove the air via the water displacement method or vacuum-sealer.

5. Submerge in the heated water bath and set the timer for 1 hour.

6. When steaks are ready, remove the steaks and pat dry with clean paper towels.

7. Heat a skillet and sear each side of the steaks until crispy. Let the steaks rest for a minute before serving with the sauce.

For the Sauce

1. In a medium skillet, heat the olive oil over medium high heat. When hot, add the onion, pepper, and salt and sauté until caramelized. Add pineapple and continue to cook until liquid has evaporated.

2. Transfer the mixture to a blender and puree until smooth.

Spicy Tofu

Serves 4

Extra equipment: Fry pan

Ingredients

1 lb. firm tofu, cut into 12 pieces

¼ cup soy sauce

¼ cup sugar

2 tablespoons mirin

2 tablespoons water

1 tablespoon crushed ginger

1 tablespoon crushed garlic

1 small red chilli, thinly sliced

Instructions

1. Set your sous-vide machine to 180°F

2. Shallow-fry the tofu pieces until the outsides are golden brown.

3. Combine all other ingredients over a medium heat until the sugar is dissolved.

4. Place all ingredients into a ziplock or vacuum-seal bag and seal using the water displacement method or a vacuum-sealer.

5. Cook for 4 hours, and serve over rice or noodles.

Beef Short Ribs

Serves 4

Ingredients

3 lbs. beef short-ribs
2 tablespoon canola oil
1 tablespoon butter, divided
Salt and pepper
3 cloves of garlic, crushed
2 bay leaves
3 sprigs of thyme
3 sprigs of parsley
2 cups red wine

2 cups beef or veal stock
1 shallot
1 tablespoon olive oil
1 bay leaf
1 teaspoon black peppercorns
1 star anise
2 tablespoon sugar
2 tablespoon butter

Instructions

1. Prepare the short ribs by trimming the excess fat. Season the short ribs well with salt.

2. Heat a cast iron pan on medium heat until it is hot and smoking. Add the oil and sear the ribs on all sides.

3. When the ribs are a dark brown, remove from the heat and generously season with freshly cracked pepper. Place the ribs into a ziplock or vacuum bag. Add the garlic and bouquet garni, and a tablespoon of butter to the bag.

4. Set your sous vide machine at 145°F. Place the ribs into the water bath and cook for 20-40 minutes depending on how well done you like your ribs.

5. When ready, remove the bag from the water and immediately transfer to an ice bath. Submerge for a minute.

6. To serve, place the ribs on a rack on top of a baking sheet and glaze with the sauce. Place the ribs into the oven and bake until the internal temperature reaches 131°F. Make sure to continue glazing the ribs every 10 minutes.

For the Sauce

1. In a medium skillet, heat the olive oil. When hot, sauté the shallot until soft.

2. Deglaze the pan with the wine and add stir in the beef stock. Add the sugar, bay leaf, peppercorns, and star anise to the pan and reduce.

3. Strain the solids and return the sauce to the pot and continue to reduce until sauce has thickened slightly. Whisk in the butter until the sauce is smooth. Season with salt and sugar to taste.

Viet-Style Chicken Skewers

Serves 4

Ingredients

1 lb. chicken breast or thighs, chopped into

1 inch pieces

1 stalk fresh lemongrass, chopped and smashed

2 Tablespoons fish sauce

2 Tablespoons coconut sugar

1/2 teaspoon salt

1 tablespoon chili-garlic sauce

Instructions

1. Set your sous vide machine to 150°F.

2. In a blender, combine the lemongrass, sugar, fish sauce, and salt. Process until ingredients are mixed and lemongrass finely chopped.

3. In a medium sized bowl, add your chicken pieces and pour the marinade over the chicken. Set aside to marinate in the refrigerator for at least 20 min.

4. When ready, skewer 3 - 4 pieces of chicken on each skewer, making sure to cushion the pointy end of the skewer with a piece of chicken.

5. Place the skewers into a ziplock or vacuum-seal bag. Pour in the remaining marinade. Use the water displacement method or vacuum-sealer to remove as much air as possible and seal.

6. Place the bag in the bath and set the timer for 45 minutes.

7. When the chicken is ready, remove from the bath and brush with chili garlic sauce. Place the skewers onto a baking sheet and broil for a few minutes, or grill them on a barbeque.

Homemade Corned Beef

Serves 12

Ingredients

3 quarts cold water, divided into 3 equal parts

1 cup sea salt

½ cup brown sugar

2 tablespoons curing salt

2 whole cinnamon sticks

1 tablespoon green cardamom pods

1 ½ teaspoons vanilla extract

1 ½ teaspoons ground ginger

1 ½ teaspoons whole cloves

1 ½ teaspoons allspice berries

1 ½ teaspoons black peppercorns

2 whole bay leaves

1 teaspoon mustard seeds

7-8 lbs. beef brisket, trimmed

Instructions

1. In a small saucepan, add 2 cups water and stir in the salts, sugar, and spices over medium to medium-high heat. Simmer the mixture while stirring to dissolve the salt and sugar. When the salts and sugar are dissolved, remove from the heat and cool.

2. When the mixture is cooled, stir into the remaining 2 ½ quarts of water into a container large enough to hold the entire brisket. Taste the curing liquid and adjust the flavoring according to your tastes.

3. Lower the brisket into the curing liquid, making sure that it is completely submerged. Cover your container and place in the refrigerator. Let the brisket brine for at least 5 days, or up to a maximum of 10 days.

4. When ready, remove your corned beef from the brine and pat dry with clean paper towels.

5. Set your sous vide machine to 140°F.

6. Place your brined brisket into a zip lock or vacuum-seal bag and use the water displacement method to release as much air as possible before sealing.

7. Submerge the sealed bag into the water bath and cook for at least 48 hours, or up to 60 hours.

8. When ready, remove the cooked corned beef from the bath and bag and

rinse under running water to remove any extra salt. Pat dry.

9. Serve as a side, or in your favorite sandwich

Orange & Bourbon-Glazed Chicken Wings

Serves 4

Ingredients

1 lb. chicken wings

¼ teaspoon salt

¼ teaspoon pepper

½ cup orange juice

½ cup brown sugar

Splash of tart cherry juice

Dash orange bitters

Zest of 1 orange

2 Tablespoons bourbon

1 Tablespoon Sriracha

2 Tablespoons vegetable oil

Instructions

1. Set your sous vide machine to 140°F.

2. Season the chicken wings with salt & pepper and place into a zip lock or vacuum-seal bag. Use the water displacement method or vacuum-sealer to release as much air as possible, seal.

3. Submerge into the hot water bath and set a timer for 90 minutes.

4. Meanwhile, combine the orange juice, orange zest, brown sugar, cherry juice, and orange bitters in a

small saucepan over medium heat. Reduce the sauce until thick.

5. Remove the sauce from the heat and stir in bourbon and sriracha.

6. When the wings are ready, remove from the bath and bag, and pat dry with clean paper towels.

7. Heat 2 Tablespoons vegetable oil in a skillet over medium-high heat and brown the wings on both sides.

8. In a large mixing bowl, toss the wings in the glaze to coat evenly.

Philly Cheese Steak

Serves 2

Ingredients

8 oz. flank steak

¼ teaspoon salt

¼ teaspoon pepper

¼ teaspoon garlic powder

1 green Bell pepper, julienne

1 yellow or red Bell pepper, julienne

1 white onion, thinly-sliced

3 garlic cloves, minced

2 Tablespoons olive oil

A pinch of salt

4-8 slices of provolone cheese

2 sandwich rolls

Instructions

1. Set your sous vide machine to 131°F.

2. Generously season both sides of your flanks steak with salt, pepper, and garlic powder.

3. Place the flank steak into a zip lock or vacuum-seal bag and use the water displacement method or vacuum-sealer to release as much air as possible from the bag, seal.

4. Place into the heated bath and set a timer for 90 minutes.

5. Meanwhile, heat olive oil in a skillet over medium-high heat. When hot, sauté the vegetables and season with salt. When the vegetables are tender and caramelized, remove from heat and set aside.

6. When the steak is ready, remove from the bath and pat dry with clean paper towels.

7. Sear the steak in a hot pan greased with oil until both sides are caramelized.

8. Slice the steak against the grain and then into 1 inch, or bite sized, pieces.

9. Add the bite-size pieces of meat into the same pan you seared the steak in, and cook while stirring, until there is no pink left. Lower heat and spread the meat into one layer in the pan and top with cheese, allow the cheese to melt undisturbed.

10. To serve, slice the bread in half lengthwise and toast under the broiler until golden and crust is crispy. Remove

your rolls from the oven and top with a
portion of the meat

Indian-Style Rack of Lamb

Serves 4

Ingredients

1-1.5 lb. rack of lamb

2 teaspoons garam masala spice blend

½ teaspoon salt

½ teaspoon pepper

Instructions

1. Set your sous vide machine to 135°F.

2. Generously season your lamb rack with salt and pepper. Rub the garam masala into the meat, making sure to completely coat the meat with the spice.

3. Place lamb rack, meat-first with the bone upwards into a zip lock or vacuum-seal bag. Using the water displacement method or vacuum-seal, release as much air as possible and seal.

4. Place in the bath and set timer for 1.5 hours.

5. When ready, remove the meat from the bath and pat dry with clean paper towels.

6. Heat a cast iron pan until smoking. Sear the rack of lamb on all sides until golden brown and caramelized.

7. To serve, slice between the bones to get individual lollipops.

Mediterranean Chicken Roulade

Serves 2

Ingredients

2 chicken breasts

¼ cup soft goat cheese

¼ cup julienned roasted red peppers

½ cup arugula

6 slices prosciutto

Salt and pepper

1 tablespoon oil

Instructions

1. Set your sous vide machine to 155°F.

2. Pat your chicken breast dry with clean paper towels and loosely wrap each breast with plastic wrap.

3. With a mallet or another flat, heavy, object, pound the chicken until it is about ¼ of an inch thick.

4. Season the chicken with salt and pepper on both sides. Then spread a tablespoon of goat cheese on one side and add a column of red pepper and arugula onto each breast.

5. Roll the chicken breast, making sure to tuck the ingredients inwards as you go. Set aside.

6. On a flat surface, lay your prosciutto, overlapping the edges a bit. Place your chicken roll on top and roll up.

7. Place the wrapped roulades into a zip lock or vacuum-seal bag, making sure to keep a gap between the two roulades. Remove as much air as possible from the bag using the water displacement method or a vacuum-sealer.

8. Submerge the roulades into the bath and set the timer for 90 minutes.

9. When ready, take the chicken out of the bath and bag and pat dry with paper towels.

10. Heat a skillet with a tablespoon of oil until hot and sear the roulade on all sides. Slice and serve.

Shrimp in Creamy White Wine Sauce

Serves 4

Ingredients

1 lb. shrimp, shelled and de-veined

2 cups heavy cream

1 cup white wine

1 cup baby arugula

4 cloves garlic, minced

2 tsp olive oil

Salt and Pepper

¼ cup pine nuts, toasted

1 tablespoon of butter

Instructions

1. Set your sous vide machine to 137.5°F.

2. Place shrimp, garlic, salt and pepper, and olive oil into a zip lock or vacuum-seal bag. Use the water displacement method or vacuum-sealer to release as much air as possible.

3. Submerge the bag into the heated bath and set timer for 30 minutes.

4. Meanwhile, combine the cream, wine, butter, and pinch of salt in a skillet over medium high heat.

5. Bring ingredients to a boil and then reduce heat to medium low. Let sauce simmer, stirring it occasionally.

6. When the sauce is reduced and thick enough to coat the back of the spoon, remove the sauce from the heat.

7. When the shrimp is done, reheat the sauce and pour the contents into the cream sauce. Stir to coat the shrimp evenly with the sauce. Add the arugula and stir until wilted.

8. Serve over pasta or rice, and garnish with the toasted pine nuts for extra crunch.

Lemon Glazed Scallops

Serves 6

Ingredients

2 pounds scallops, muscle removed

2 Meyer lemons

Salt and Pepper to taste

2 tablespoons butter

2 tablespoon green onions, finely chopped

Pinch red chili flakes

4 tablespoons dry sherry

½ cup orange juice

2 teaspoons honey

Instructions

1. Set your sous vide machine to 122°F.

2. Divide your scallops between two zip lock and vacuum-seal bags. Place 2 slices of Meyer lemon per bag and season with salt and pepper. Seal bag using water displacement method or a vacuum-sealer. Place in the water and cook 30 minutes.

3. While scallops are cooking, make sauce. Heat butter in skillet over medium-high heat. Add white part of scallion with chili flakes and cook until soft. Remove scallion from skillet and set aside.

4. In a small bowl, juice and zest 1 lemon (reserve a bit of zest for garnish). Stir in the orange juice.

5. When the scallops are ready, remove and pat dry.

6. Heat the same skillet again over high heat and then gently sear the scallops on each side, about 90 seconds.

7. Remove scallops from skillet and deglaze skillet with sherry. Stir in the lemon and orange juice mixture. Add in the sautéed white scallions and then bring to a boil. Reduce the sauce until it becomes a thick glaze, stir in the honey until well combined.

8. Plate the scallops and spoon the lemon sauce on top. Garnish with green scallions and additional zest. Serve immediately.

Fragrant Tuna Carpaccio

Serves 4

Ingredients

2 tuna steaks

Kosher salt

Freshly ground black pepper

2 tablespoons extra-virgin olive oil

Aromatics: fresh thyme, dill, parsley, thinly sliced shallots, lemon zest

½ cup white sesame seeds

2 teaspoons vegetable oil

Instructions

1. Season tuna generously with salt and pepper on all sides.

2. Place tuna in a single layer in a ziplock or vacuum-seal bag. In the bag, add olive oil and your choice of aromatics. Remove as much air as you can with the water displacement method or vacuum-sealer and seal. Place the bags in the refrigerator, and let the tuna marinade for at least 30 minutes or overnight.

3. Set the temperature of your sous vide machine to 115°F and submerge the tuna steaks into the preheated water bath. Cook for 30 to 45 minutes for one-inch filets, or 45 minutes to an hour for filets up to two inches thick.

4. When ready, remove the fish from the water and the bag and pat dry. Heat a skillet with a tablespoon of oil until hot and then sear the fish on all sides for about 1-2 minutes.

5. Slice and serve.

Ratatouille

Extra equipment: Fry pan

Ingredients

For the vegetables
2 zucchinis, sliced in ¼ inches lengthways
1 large red bell pepper, sliced into 2-inch strips
1 eggplant, sliced into ¼ inch rounds
1 onion
4 cloves garlic
8 basil leaves

Salt and cracked black pepper
Olive oil
For the sauce
2 tablespoons olive oil
1 onion, diced
2 cloves garlic, finely cut
2 tins diced tomatoes
Salt and cracked black pepper to taste
10-12 basil leaves

Instructions

1. Set your sous vide machine to 185°F.

2. Place vegetables all in their own bags, adding a clove of crushed garlic, 2 basil leaves, a pinch of salt and pepper and a drizzle of olive oil to each.

3. Seal the bags using the water displacement method or a vacuum-sealer and submerge in the water bath.

4. After one hour, remove the zucchini and peppers. After another hour, remove the eggplant and onions

5. Heat the olive oil on a medium heat in a fry-pan. When it starts to shimmer slightly, add the onions and garlic, stirring continuously to avoid burning.

6. When onions have softened, add the tomato and raise the heat until the sauce begins to bubble. Lower heat, add salt and pepper to taste, and simmer for a minimum of 40 minutes. When the sauce thickens, taste a small amount. If it isn't your desired sweetness, add some water and continue to simmer.

7. Cut the vegetables into ½ inch pieces and put into a large bowl, removing basil leaves and garlic cloves. Pour your sauce over the vegetables and mix until everything it combined.

8. Tear up 10-12 basil leaves and stir through before serving, adding salt and pepper to taste.

Mediterranean Herbed Octopus

Serves 2

Ingredients

1 whole octopus

1 tablespoon olive oil

2 sprigs thyme

1 sprig rosemary

Pinch of sea salt

Fresh Lemon, to serve

Instructions

1. Remove the entrails, eyes and beak of the octopus and clean.

2. Set your sous vide machine to 167°F.

3. Pat the octopus dry and place in double-bagged ziplock or vacuum-seal bags. Add olive oil, thyme, rosemary and sea salt into the bags.

4. Seal the bag using the water displacement method or a vacuum-sealer and submerge in the water bath for 8 hours.

5. When ready, remove the octopus from the bag and discard the liquid. Gently rub off the loose skin and then separate the tentacles. Carefully pat each of them dry.

6. To serve, heat a skillet with oil and sear the octopus for a few seconds until the exterior is slightly crispy.

7. Serve with fresh lemon for squeezing.

Italian Sausages with Grapes

Serves 4

Ingredients

2 ½ cups seedless red grapes, stems removed

1 tablespoon fresh rosemary, chopped

2 tablespoons butter

4 sweet or hot Italian sausages

2 tablespoons balsamic vinegar

Salt and freshly ground black pepper

Instructions

1. Set your sous vide machine to 160°F.

2. In a ziplock or vacuum-seal bag, place the grapes, rosemary, butter and sausages in one layer. Remove as much air as possible with the water displacement method or a vacuum-sealer.

3. Place the sausages into the preheated water bath and set a timer for 1 hour.

4. When ready, heat a skillet on medium high heat with a small pat of butter. Sear the sausages for about 2-3 minutes on each side, or until skin is crispy. Remove and set aside.

5. In the same skillet, pour in the rest of the bagged contents and simmer. Add in the balsamic vinegar and continue to simmer for 3-4 minutes on medium high heat, or until the sauce has reduced slightly.

6. To serve, place the sausages and spoon the grape sauce on top.

Spicy Braised Swordfish

Serves 4

Ingredients

1 lb. swordfish steaks

2 teaspoons soy sauce

2 teaspoons rice wine vinegar

1 teaspoon brown sugar

½ teaspoon sesame oil

2 chopped spring onions

1 tablespoon ginger, finely minced

1 teaspoon toasted sesame seeds

1 teaspoon chili sauce, like Sriracha

Cilantro sprigs, for garnish

1 red chili pepper, sliced and seeds removed

Lime wedges to serve

Instructions

1. Set your sous vide machine to 140°F.

2. Place your fish, soy sauce, rice wine vinegar, sugar, sesame oil, spring onions, chili pepper, and minced ginger in a ziplock or vacuum-seal bag.

3. Remove as much air as possible from the bag by using the water displacement method or vacuum-sealer. Place the bag into the water bath and set timer for 30 minutes.

4. When ready, remove from bath and tip everything onto a serving plate.

5. Garnish with a sprinkle of sesame seeds and then drizzle chili sauce on top for extra spice. Serve with cilantro leaves and a lime wedge.

Honey Glazed Duck Breast

Serves 4

Ingredients

4 boneless duck breasts

¼ teaspoon cinnamon

¼ teaspoon smoked paprika

¼ teaspoon chipotle Chile pepper or cayenne pepper

1 teaspoon honey

Salt and pepper to taste

Instructions

1. Set your sous vide machine to 135°F.

2. Gently score the skin in a crosshatch pattern and sprinkle salt on both sides.

3. Heat up a large skillet over high heat and sear the duck, skin side first. Sear until the skin turns a golden brown. Remove from the pan and set aside.

4. In a small bowl, combine all the spices. Season the duck breast generously with the spice mix.

5. Place the duck breasts into a zip lock or vacuum-seal bag and add the honey. Remove the air by using the water displacement method or vacuum-sealer. Submerge the duck into the prepared bath for 1-3.5 hours.

6. When ready, remove the duck breasts from the bath and the bag. Pat dry.

7. Sear the duck breast, skin side down first, on a hot skillet until skin is crispy. Flip and sear the other side until golden brown, about 1-2 minutes. Slice and serve.

Crispy Pork Belly

Serves 4

Ingredients

2 lbs. pork belly

1 bunch green onions

10 cloves garlic

¼c/60 ml soy sauce

3 Thai chilies, dried

1 teaspoon minced ginger

1/2 teaspoon white pepper

Oil for frying

Instructions

1. Set your sous vide machine to 155°F.

2. Place your pork, green onion, 2 garlic cloves, and white pepper into a zip lock or vacuum-seal bag. Use the water displacement or vacuum-sealer to remove as much air as possible and then seal.

3. Submerge this in the bath for 24 hours. Cover the container with plastic wrap to prevent too much heat from escaping and top off with more water over time.

4. When done, remove the bag from the bath and then separate the pork and liquids into two bowls.

5. Pour the cooking liquid into a sauce pan and cook over medium high heat until it has reduced to about 1 cup.

6. In another pan, heat a small amount of oil. When hot, quickly sauté the remaining cloves of garlic and the Thai chilies until fragrant. Add in the reduced cooking liquid and honey and then continue to cook down until sauce is syrupy. Set aside.

7. In a thick bottom pot or a cast iron skillet, heat your frying oil to 350°F. Cut your pork belly into thick cubs and then thread it onto a bamboo skewer. Deep fry until golden and crispy on the outside. Remove and dab off any excess oil with some paper towels.

8. To serve, drizzle the skewer with the sauce.

Homestyle Shepherd's Pie

Serves 4

Ingredients

2 pound boneless lamb leg
Salt and freshly ground black pepper
4 cloves garlic, peeled and smashed
1 sprig fresh thyme, leaves removed from stem, plus 2 tablespoons (6g) chopped
1 sprig fresh rosemary, leaves removed from stem, plus 1 tablespoon chopped
2 tablespoons extra virgin olive oil
4 carrots, peeled and chopped

2 parsnips, peeled and chopped
4 celery stalks, chopped
1 medium onion, chopped
2 tablespoons all-purpose flour
4 cups chicken stock
4 medium russet potatoes, peeled and quartered
4 tablespoons unsalted butter, at room temperature
½ cup whole milk, at room temperature

Instructions

1. Set your sous vide machine to 140°F.

2. Season the lamb with salt and pepper and place it into a ziplock or vacuum-seal bag. In the bag, add garlic, whole thyme leaves, and whole rosemary leaves.

3. Use the water displacement method or a vacuum-sealer to remove the air in the bag and then seal. Submerge the bag in the water bath and set the timer for 24 hours. Cover the water bath with plastic wrap to minimize evaporation and top off the bath with more water over time.

4. When the lamb is almost done, heat olive oil in a large thick bottom pot over medium high heat. Sauté the carrots, parsnips, celery, and onion and season with salt.

Continue to cook, stirring occasionally, until onions are translucent.

5. Add in the flour, chopped thyme, and chopped rosemary and continue to cook. Stir constantly until herbs are fragrant and then gradually pour in chicken stock while stirring.

6. Increase the temperature to high and bring the stock to a boil before reducing the heat to medium low. Continue to cook, stirring occasionally, until vegetables are soft.

7. Remove from the pot from the heat and let it cool, covered in the refrigerator until the lamb is completely finished.

8. When the lamb is done, remove it and shred it with two forks. Stir it into the vegetable mixture and then tip it into an oven safe dish. Cover the top with mashed potatoes and bake under the broiler for 5-8 minutes or until the potatoes are crisp and golden brown.

Chicken & Seafood Paella

Serves 4

Ingredients

1 lb. boneless, skinless chicken breasts
½ pound chorizo, sliced into rounds
2 tablespoons olive oil
3 cups rice
½ large onion, finely chopped
1 bay leaf
½ teaspoon smoked paprika
1 pinch saffron threads

¼ cup wine
5 ¼ cups chicken stock
1 pound shrimp, shelled and de veined
1 cup frozen peas, thawed
8 frozen artichoke hearts, thawed and chopped
24 small mussels, cleaned
6 strips roasted red pepper

Instructions

1. Set your sous vide machine to 145°F.

2. Season your chicken breast with salt and pepper and then place it in a ziplock of vacuum-seal bag with the chorizo. Remove the air by using the water displacement method or a vacuum-sealer.

3. Submerge in the prepared water bath and cook for 45 minutes.

4. When done remove from water, and chill in an ice bath. Shred the chicken with two forks and slice the chorizo into rounds.

5. Set your sous vide machine to 131 F. Place your shrimp into a zip lock or a vacuum-seal bag and remove the air. Submerge in the water bath and cook for 15 min.

6. Preheat the oven to 450°F.

7. In a large cast iron skillet, heat the oil over medium high heat. When hot, sauté the onion until fragrant and slightly translucent. Then add in the rice, bay leaf, paprika and saffron.

8. Cook, stirring constantly until rice becomes opaque then add wine, then add chicken stock and stir well. Stir in the cooked chorizo rounds. Reduce heat, cover and continue to cook until rice is done, about 20 minutes.

9. Stir in the chicken, peas, and artichoke hearts into rice. Press mussels into the rice, hinge side down and then arrange the strips of red pepper on top of rice.

10. When the shrimp is ready, remove it from the water and the bag and then place the shrimp on top of the rice. Place the skillet into the hot oven and cook for 5 minutes.

11. Discard any un-opened mussels before serving.

Fish Tacos with Pineapple Salsa

Serves 4

Ingredients

1 ½ lbs. cod	A pinch of chili powder
½ teaspoon adobo seasoning	Juice of 1 lime
½ teaspoon chili powder	A pinch of salt
½ fresh pineapple	1 tablespoon vegetable oil
¼ cup chopped fresh mint	Soft flour tortillas, 6-inch diameter
1 teaspoon sugar	1 avocado, peeled, seeded and sliced
1 tablespoon chopped red onion	2 tablespoons sour cream

Instructions

1. Set your sous vide machine to 134.6°F.

2. Season fish with adobo and chili powder and then place into a ziplock or a vacuum-seal bag. Remove the air using the water displacement method or a vacuum-sealer and then seal.

3. Submerge into the prepared water bath and then and cook for 30 minutes.

4. To prepare the pineapple salsa, heat grill and grill the pineapple until warm and slightly caramelized. Dice the pineapple and transfer to a bowl with the mint, sugar, red onion, chili powder, lime juice and salt. Toss to mix.

5. When fish is done, remove the bag from water and then the fish. Pat dry with paper towels.

6. Heat oil in large skillet over high heat and then sear the fish, 1 minute on each side. Transfer onto a clean cutting board and cut the fish into vertical strips. Heat the tortillas according to package directions.

7. To assemble the tacos, top each tortilla with ½ teaspoon of sour cream, sliced avocados, and the pineapple salsa. Serve immediately

Cornbread

Serves 8

Ingredients

½ cup coarse-ground cornmeal

½ cup all-purpose flour

1 tablespoon granulated sugar

1 teaspoon baking powder

Pinch of salt

⅛ teaspoon baking soda

½ cup sour cream

1 large egg

2 tablespoons unsalted butter, melted

½ cup fresh corn kernels

Instructions

1. Set your sous vide machine to 195°F and then grease 4 glass jars with non-stick oil spray or butter.

2. In a large mixing bowl, whisk together the cornmeal, flour, sugar, baking powder, salt, and baking soda.

3. In another bowl beat the egg with the sour cream and then incorporate it into the cornmeal mixture. Fold in the corn kernels.

4. Divide the batter between the jars, making sure to fill each jar only half full. Firmly tap each jar on the counter top to remove any air bubbles.

5. Seal the jars, making sure to leave it slightly loose to allow air pressure to escape. Place jars into the water bath and cook for 3 hours.

6. When done, remove the jars from the water bath and let them cool at room temperature on a cooling rack with the lids removed.

7. To serve, run a sharp knife along the edge of the jar, then run a knife around the sides of the jars, and invert to un-mold the loaves. Slice each loaf into two or three pieces and serve with some butter on the side.

Fried Chicken & Waffles

Serves 6

Ingredients

2.2 lbs. boneless, skinless chicken breast

¼ cup buttermilk

6 teaspoons honey

1 ¾ cups beer

1 egg

⅔ cup all-purpose flour

1 teaspoon paprika

1 teaspoon garlic powder

Salt and Pepper to taste

¼ cup vegetable oil for frying

6 of your favorite waffles

Instructions

1. Set your sous vide machine to 145.4°F.

2. Place your chicken breasts in a ziplock or a vacuum-seal bag and add salt, pepper, and buttermilk. Remove the air by using the water displacement method or a vacuum-sealer and then seal. Shuffle the chicken around to make sure it is laying in one single layer and there is little to no overlap.

3. Cook in the prepared water bath for 45 minutes.

4. When the chicken is almost ready, mix the flour, paprika, garlic powder, salt and pepper in a shallow dish.

5. About 10 minutes before chicken is done, begin heating your oil in a large cast iron skillet to 350°F.

6. 5 minutes before chicken is done, make the batter by mixing flour with egg and beer. Stir gently until there is no more lumps.

7. When the chicken is ready, remove the chicken from the water and the bag and pat dry. Coat each piece with the seasoned flour and then dip it into the batter. Shake gently to remove any excess batter. Coat the chicken breast one more time with the season flour and then carefully place it into the hot oil.

8. Fry until the batter turns a nice golden brown and is crispy.

9. Serve the crispy chicken with a waffle and then drizzle some honey on top.

Eggplant Lasagna

Serves 4

Ingredients

2 pounds eggplant, peeled and sliced into thick rounds

2 teaspoons kosher salt

1 ½ cups prepared tomato sauce

3 oz. fresh mozzarella, thinly sliced

2 oz. grated Parmesan cheese

4 oz. grated Italian Blend cheese

¼ cup chopped fresh basil

1 tablespoon seasoned breadcrumbs

Instructions

1. Set your sous vide machine to 183°F.

2. Rub the eggplant slices with salt, place them in a colander in the sink, and let the excess liquid drain for about 30 minutes. Rinse off the salt and pat dry with paper towels.

3. Arrange the eggplant slices in a ziplock or vacuum-seal bag. Try to keep it in one layer or only overlapping slightly.

4. Spoon in half the tomato sauce and then layer the mozzarella on top. Then sprinkle half the Parmesan, followed by the basil. Repeat this step until all ingredients, except ½ cup of tomato sauce, is used.

5. Carefully seal the bag by using the water displacement or a vacuum-sealer, try to keep the bag as flat as possible. Submerge in the water bath and cook for 3 hours. If the bag inflates

during the cooking process, carefully remove it and open the bag to release the air. Reseal and submerge in the water bath again.

6. When done, open a small corner of the bag and drain out the cooking liquid.

7. Lay the bag flat on a serving platter and gently slide the layered eggplant into place. Let it rest and then gently tip the plate the remove excess liquid. Top the eggplant with remaining tomato sauce and then sprinkling breadcrumbs and Parmesan cheese on top.

8. Finish off the eggplant under the broiler until the breadcrumbs are golden

Parmesan Fennel

Serves 4

Ingredients

2 large bulbs fennel, trimmed, washed and quartered through root

1/2 cup chicken stock

1 tablespoon butter

1 oz. Parmesan cheese

Salt and Pepper to taste

Instructions

1. Set your sous vide machine to 183°F.

2. Place the fennel in to a ziplock or vacuum-seal bag with the stock and butter. Remove the air by using the water displacement method or a vacuum-sealer and then seal. Cook submerged in the water bath for 3-4 hours.

3. When the fennel is ready, remove from the water bath and bag, and drain off the excess liquid. Meanwhile, heat a cast iron skillet over high heat.

4. When the skillet is hot, sear one side of each fennel wedge. Sprinkle parmesan on top and serve immediately.

Cauliflower Alfredo

Serves 2

Ingredients

2 cups (400g) chopped cauliflower florets

1/2 cup double-strength chicken or vegetable stock

2 garlic cloves, crushed

2 tablespoons milk

2 tablespoons butter

Salt and pepper

Instructions

1. Set your sous vide machine to 181°F.

2. Place all your ingredients into a ziplock or vacuum-seal bag. Squeeze out some air and then fold the edge of the bag over to seal. Place the bag into the prepared water bath and clip the edge to the container or pot.

3. Cook for 2 hours.

4. When ready, pour the contents of the bag into a food processor and blend until smooth and creamy. Season with more salt and pepper, and then serve over you r favorite pasta.

Cheesy Grits

Serves 2

Ingredients

1 cup old fashioned grits

1 cup cream

3 cups chicken stock

2 tablespoons butter, cubed

2 oz. grated cheddar cheese

Paprika and extra cheese for garnish

Instructions

1. Set your sous vide machine to 180°F.

2. In a medium mixing bowl, whisk together the cream and stock and then add in your grits. Continue to whisk until the mixture is no longer lumpy. Add the butter to the grits and stir.

3. Transfer the mixture to a ziplock or vacuum-seal bag and remove the air by using the water displacement method or a vacuum-sealer. Seal shut.

4. Submerge the bag under hot water. Make sure to lay the bag flat on the bottom of the water container to prevent lumps. If lumps in the grits do form, take it out of the water bag and then use your hands or a wooden spoon to disperse the lumps.

5. Cook for 2-3 hours, or until the grits have absorbed most of the liquid.

6. When the grits are done, pour it into a large mixing bowl and then whisk in the cheese. Season with salt and pepper to taste.

7. To serve, sprinkle more cheese and some paprika.

Herbed Butter Halibut

Serves 4

Ingredients

4 halibut fillets

Kosher salt

2 tablespoons butter

1-2 sprigs of thyme, dill, and parsley

1 tablespoon shallots, thinly sliced

2 teaspoons vegetable oil

Instructions

1. Generously season the halibut on all sides with salt and pepper.

2. Place the halibut fillets in a single layer inside one or more ziplock or vacuum-seal bags.

3. In the bags, add the butter, herbs, and shallots. Seal and let the fillets marinate in the refrigerator for at least 30 minutes or overnight.

4. Set the temperature on your sous vide machine to 130°F. Remove the halibut from the refrigerator while you wait for the water to preheat.

5. Remove all the air from the bag using the water displacement method or a vacuum-sealer and then place the halibut to the water bath. Cook for 30 to 45 minutes for one-inch filets, or 45 minutes to an hour for filets up to two inches thick.

6. When ready, remove the fish from the water and the bag and pat dry. Heat a skillet with a small pat of butter and sear the fish until it becomes a light golden color. Serve.

Buttery Lemon Mushrooms

Serves 4

Ingredients

10 oz. white mushrooms, cleaned and quartered

3 tablespoons olive oil

1 oz. dry sherry

½ teaspoon dried thyme

1 teaspoon Worcestershire sauce

1 bay leaf

1 strip lemon peel

Salt and pepper to taste

Dash garlic powder

Instructions

1. Set your sous vide machine to 185°F.

2. Place mushrooms into ziplock or vacuum-seal bag. Add olive oil, sherry, thyme, Worcestershire, bay leaf, lemon peel, salt and pepper and garlic powder. Seal and gently shake to mix ingredients.

3. Remove as much air as possible by using the water displacement method or a vacuum-sealer. Place in the preheated water and cook 1 hour.

4. When ready, remove mushrooms from cooking water and serve, or let it cool in the juices in the bag and store it in the refrigerator overnight.

Crispy Chicken Wings

Serves 2

Ingredients

2 lbs. chicken wings

½ teaspoon salt

½ teaspoon pepper

2 Tablespoons cornstarch

1 cup sauce of your choice

Oil for frying

Instructions

1. Set your sous vide machine to 150°F.

2. Season your wings with salt and pepper and place them into a zip lock or a vacuum-seal bag. Use your hands to shuffle the wings into one layer and then use the water displacement method or a vacuum-sealer to remove as much air as possible.

3. Submerge the wings in the water bath for 2 hours and 30 minutes.

4. When done remove wings from the bath and the bag and then pat dry with paper towels. Let the wings air dry to room temperature on a wire rack.

5. When dried, toss the wings with the cornstarch and then let it chill overnight in the refrigerator uncovered to increase dryness.

6. When ready, heat oil to 350-375°F and then fry the wings for 5 minutes on each side or until golden. Remove from the oil and pat off the excess oil with a paper towel. At this point, you can eat the wings as is with some salt and pepper, or toss it in your favorite sauce.

Classic Stuffing

Serves 4

Ingredients

5 stick of celery, diced

4 cups turkey Stock

2 white onions, diced

1 cup dried cranberries

2 large eggs

2 large French baguettes, torn into bite-size pieces

1 package of bacon, cut into cubes

1 tablespoon of fresh sage, chopped

2 large garlic cloves, diced

Salt and pepper to taste

Instructions

1. Set your sous vide machine to 161.5°F.

2. In a medium sized skillet, cook your bacon until just done and not crispy. Transfer the bacon onto a plate, but save the fat in the skillet.

3. Add the onions, celery and garlic to the bacon fat and cook until the vegetables are fragrant and slightly tender.

4. In a large bowl, whisk the eggs. Stir in the turkey stock, veggies, bacon, sage, salt/pepper, and cranberries until well combined.

Add the bread into the mix and toss to coat.

5. Pour the bread mixture into a large ziplock or vacuum-seal bag and remove all the air by using the water displacement method or a vacuum-sealer. Cook submerged in the water bath for 1 hour.

6. When the stuffing is almost ready, preheat the oven to broil.

7. When done the stuffing is done, transfer it to a baking dish and place it under the broiler for 15 minutes, or until the top is lightly browned.

Desserts

There's unlikely to be anyone at the table who turns their nose up at desserts, except perhaps the one who has to make them! Preparing your ingredients sous vide can be done in advance in a lot of situations, and this means more time to enjoy the last bit of dinner with the people around you - not in the company of a piping hot oven. From the fruit lovers to the chocolate addicts, there is a sous vide dessert recipe for just about everyone, now it's just a matter of deciding which one to make.

Soft Cranberry Pears

Serves 4

Ingredients

2 oz. water

6 tablespoons cranberry jam

¼ cup sugar

1 teaspoon salt

4 pears, rinsed, peeled, cored, halved

Instructions

1. Set your sous vide machine to 185°F.

2. Whisk together jam, sugar, salt and a little water to make the sauce. Add pears and toss to coat.

3. Place the pears into a large ziplock bag or a vacuum-seal bag and pour in the sauce. Remove all the air with the water displacement method or a vacuum-sealer. Seal and submerge the bag in the water bath and cook for 1 hour or until the pears are tender with a bit of bite.

4. When done, remove from the pouch and serve with a scoop of vanilla ice-cream.

Rice & Raisin Pudding

Serves 2

Ingredients

1 cup Arborio rice

1 ½ cups skim milk

1 tablespoon butter

¼ cup golden raisins

¼ cup maple syrup or to taste

¼ teaspoon ground ginger

1 teaspoon ground cinnamon

Instructions

1. Set your sous vide machine to 182°F.

2. Add all the ingredients into a large ziplock bag or a vacuum-seal bag. Remove all the air with the water displacement method or a vacuum-sealer. Seal and submerge the bag in the water bath and cook for 45 to 60 minutes or until done

3. Remove the pouch from water. Mix well and transfer into dessert bowls.

4. Serve warm or chilled.

Saffron Crème Brulee

Serves 2

Ingredients

2 cups heavy cream

½ cup sugar

4 egg yolks

4-5 strands of saffron

Instructions

1. Place a pan over low heat. Pour in the cream and cook until just warmed. Add in the saffron strands and stir. Remove from heat and wrap with cling film. Set it aside too steep for 2-3 hours.

2. After 2-3 hours, place the pan over medium heat and warm the cream again.

3. Set your sous vide machine to 185°F.

4. In a medium bowl, beat the yolks with the sugar until the sugar is dissolved. Add a little of hot cream and whisk well. Continue to add a little bit of the cream to the egg mixture until none is left. Pour the mixture into a large ziplock bag or a vacuum-seal bag. Remove all the air with the water displacement method or a vacuum-sealer. Seal and submerge the bag in the water bath and cook for 60 minutes or until done.

5. Remove the pouch from water. Pour it into a large bowl and stir before portioning it out into dessert bowls. Chill in the refrigerator until ready to serve.

6. To serve, remove from the refrigerator and sprinkle a tablespoon of sugar on top. Use a torch to melt the sugar until it is caramel brown and then serve.

Caramelized Bananas

Serves 6

Ingredients

10 small ripe firm bananas, peeled, chopped into chunks

4 whole cloves

4 sticks cinnamon

2 cups brown sugar

Whipped cream or vanilla ice cream to serve

Instructions

1. Set your sous vide machine to 176°F.

2. Add all the ingredients except vanilla ice cream into a large ziplock bag or a vacuum-seal bag. Remove all the air with the water displacement method or a vacuum-sealer. Seal and submerge the bag in the water bath and cook for 30-40 minutes or until done

3. Remove the pouch from water. Mix well and transfer into dessert bowls. Discard cloves and cinnamon.

4. Serve warm or chilled with vanilla ice cream.

Lemon & Blueberry Cheesecake

Serves 2

Ingredients

For the graham cracker crust

1 teaspoon butter for greasing the ramekins

½ cup graham crackers, crumbled

¼ cup melted butter

1 tablespoon sugar

For the cheesecake

24 oz. cream cheese

1 cup sugar

½ cup sour cream

4 eggs

Zest of 2 lemons, finely chopped

½ cup lemon juice

For topping

1 cup blueberries

2 tablespoons powdered sugar

Instructions

1. Set your sous vide machine to 176°F. Grease glass jars with butter or cooking spray.

2. In a medium mixing bowl, mix together the crust ingredients. Divide evenly between the two jars. Use the back of a spoon to flatten the crust.

3. In another bowl, cream together the cream cheese, sugar, and sour cream. Add in eggs, one at a time, making sure to fully incorporate one egg before adding the next.

Whisk in lemon juice and zest at the end. Divide this batter evenly in the two jars.

4. Seal your jars with a lid, making sure to leave it loose enough to allow trapped air pressure to escape.

5. Place the jars into the water bath and cook for 1 ½ hours.

6. When ready, remove the jars from the bath and remove the lids. Let the cheesecake cool at room

temperature before transferring it to a refrigerator to chill.

7. Serve with fresh blueberries with powdered sugar sprinkled over

Saffron Poached Pears

Serves 4

Ingredients

4 pears, peeled, cored and halved

½ teaspoon saffron

½ cup caster sugar

1 vanilla bean, cut in half, then sliced lengthways down the center

½ cup white wine

Instructions

1. Set your sous vide machine to 181.4°F.

2. Place all ingredients into a ziplock or vacuum-seal bag. Gently massage the ingredients to combine. Remove as much air as possible with the water

displacement method or a vacuum-sealer. Seal and for 1 hour.

3. To serve, place a pear half into a shallow bowl and spoon the liquid on top. Top with a large scoop of vanilla ice-cream.

Warm Peach Cobbler

Serves 6

Ingredients

1 cup self-rising flour

1 cup granulated sugar

1 cup whole milk

1 teaspoon vanilla extract

1 stick unsalted butter, melted

2 cup roughly chopped peaches

Instructions

1. Set your sous vide machine to 195°F. Generously grease 6 half-pint canning jars with non-stick oil spray or butter.

2. In a medium mixing bowl, whisk together flour and sugar. Gradually whisk in milk and vanilla until the batter is smooth. Stir in the melted butter and peaches.

3. Divide the batter between the prepared jars. Give each jar a firm tap on the counter to remove air bubbles.

4. Place lids and bands onto the jars and seal until just tight – make sure you do not over-tighten the jars to allow steam to escape. Place jars in water bath and set the timer for 3 hours.

5. When ready, place the jars onto a cooling rack and let it cool for at least 10 minutes before serving. Serve with a scoop of vanilla ice-cream.

Silky Coconut Flan

Serves 8

Ingredients

1 14 oz. can sweetened condensed milk

1 14 oz. can coconut milk

4 large eggs

1 cup sugar

½ cup water

1 cup sweetened, dried coconut flakes

Instructions

1. Set your sous vide machine to 179.6°F.

2. Prepare custard by mixing the sweetened condensed milk, coconut milk and eggs. Whisk until fully combined.

3. To make the caramel, place the sugar and water into saucepan and gently swirl to coat all the sugar with the water. Bring to boil over high heat and then reduce heat to medium and simmer 7 minutes until dark golden brown. Do not stir. Remove from heat.

4. Divide the caramel into 8 canning jars and top each with ½ cup of the coconut custard. Place the lids on top and gently place into the hot water. Water should rise about 1/2 way.

5. While flans cook, toast coconut the coconut flakes in a dry skillet over medium heat while constantly stirring. When coconut is golden brown, remove from the heat and set aside.

6. When flan is ready, remove from the hot water bath and let it cool in the refrigerator for 3 hours or overnight.

7. To serve, remove lids from containers and run sharp knife around edge of each flan. Invert the jars on top of a plate and then top with the toasted coconut.

Dairy-free Caramel Sauce

Serves 10

Ingredients

20 pitted dates

1 cup non-dairy milk

1 teaspoon vanilla

Instructions

1. Set your sous vide machine to 135°F.

2. Put all your ingredients into a ziplock or vacuum-seal bag and remove the air by using the water displacement method or a vacuum-sealer. Seal and place into the hot water bath for 2 hours.

3. When ready, pour the contents into a blender and pulse a few times before blending. Blend until smooth.

4. Let the sauce cool in the refrigerator and then serve over ice cream.

Fudgey Brownies

Serves 16

Ingredients

1 stick unsalted butter

3 oz. bittersweet chocolate, chopped

¾ cup plus 2 tablespoons granulated sugar

2 large eggs

1 teaspoon vanilla extract

⅔ cup all-purpose flour

¼ teaspoon salt

Instructions

1. Set your sous vide machine to 195°F and then grease 4 half-pint canning jars with non-stick oil spray or butter.

2. Melt the chocolate in a microwave safe bowl in 30 second intervals, stirring between each interval, until chocolate is smooth. Whisk in sugar until combined. Whisk in the eggs, one at a time, until smooth. Whisk in vanilla at the end.

3. Gently fold in flour and salt until just combined.

4. Divide the batter between the prepared jars. Each jar should be no more than half-full. Firmly tap jars on the counter to remove air bubbles.

5. Place lids and bands on jars and seal until just tight, avoid over-tightening, as air will still need to escape.

6. Place the jars in the hot water bath and set the timer for 3 hours.

7. When ready, remove the jars from the water and let them cool to room temperature on a cooling rack. When cool, run a sharp knife around the side of the jar and invert the jars to un-mold the brownies. Slice each brownie into 4 pieces.

Coconut Milk Kheer with Pistachios

Serves 6

Ingredients

5 heaping tablespoons basmati rice

2 cans coconut milk

1 cup water

3 tablespoons granulated sugar

Pinch kosher salt

10 green cardamom pods, lightly crushed

Chopped shelled pistachios, for serving

Slivered almonds, for serving

Rose water, for serving

Instructions

1. Set your sous vide machine to 180°F.

2. Divide the rice between 5 half-pint canning jars.

3. In a large bowl, whisk together coconut milk, water, sugar, and salt. Divide the mixture between the 5 jars. Add 2 cardamom pods to each jar. Place the lids and bands on the jars and seal until just tight. Do not over-tighten the jars to allow air to escape.

4. Place the jars in the hot water bath and set the timer for 3 hours.

5. When the timer goes off, remove the jars from the water bath and transfer to a cooling rack. Carefully remove the lids. Stir the pudding.

6. Let the pudding cool to room temperature before re-sealing the jars and transferring to the refrigerator. Chill for at least 4 hours.

7. Once thoroughly chilled, remove the lids and stir the pudding before serving. Top each pudding with pistachios, almonds, and a few drops of rose water. Serve chilled.

Simple Poached Pears

Serves 8

Ingredients

8 pears, peeled, cored, halved

2 cups maple syrup

4 cups white wine

4 cups water

2 cups sugar

Instructions

1. Fill and preheat the sous vide water bath to 176°F.

2. Add all the ingredients except pears to a saucepan. Place the saucepan over

medium heat. Simmer for a while until slightly thick.

3. Place the pear halves in a ziplock bag in a single layer. Do not crowd the pears and place in 2 or 3 bags if necessary.

4. Pour the sauce over the pears. vacuum-seal the pouch.

5. Submerge the bag into the water bath and cook for 60 minutes or until done

6. Remove the pouch from water. Remove the pears and serve in individual bowls.

7. Pour sauce from the pouch over the pears and serve.

Cinnamon Spiced Apples

Serves 8

Ingredients

8 tart apples, peeled, cored

Juice of 2 lemons

6 tablespoons unsalted butter

¼ cup brown sugar

4 whole fresh dates, pitted

¼ cup raisins

2 tablespoons ground cinnamon

½ teaspoon fine sea salt

½ teaspoon nutmeg, grated

¼ teaspoon vanilla extract

Fresh whipped cream or ice cream to serve

Instructions

1. Set your sous vide machine to 185°F.

2. Place your apples into a bowl and pour in the lemon juice. Toss to coat.

3. In another bowl, mix together with a fork, butter, brown sugar, dates, raisins, cinnamon, salt, nutmeg, and vanilla extract.

4. Stuff the center of the apples with the filling, making sure to firmly press it into the apples.

5. Place the apples into a large ziplock bag or a vacuum-seal bag. Remove all the air with the water displacement method or a vacuum-sealer. Seal and submerge the bag in the water bath and cook for 2 hours.

6. When done, remove the apples from the bag and place onto serving plates.

7. Serve with whipped cream or ice cream.

Blueberry Clafoutis

Serves 2

Ingredients

1 egg

¼ cup heavy cream

¼ cup almond flour

1 tablespoon granulated sugar

2 teaspoons coconut flour

¼ teaspoon baking powder

¼ teaspoon vanilla extract

A pinch salt

½ cup fresh blueberries

Instructions

1. Set your sous vide machine to 185°F.

2. In a medium mixing bowl whisk all ingredients, except the blueberries. Continue to whisk until the batter is smooth.

3. Grease your glass jars with cooking spray or vegetable oil. Divide the batter evenly between the two jars and top each with about 2 tablespoons of blueberries.

Seal the jars with the lid, making sure to keep it loose enough to allow steam and air pressure to escape.

4. Cook in the water bath for 1 hour. When done remove the jars from the bath.

5. To serve, dust some icing sugar on top and add the remaining blueberries.

Carrot Pudding

Serves 4

Ingredients

1 cup sugar or to taste

1 tablespoon almonds

½ teaspoon ground cardamom

1 pound carrots, grated

2 cups milk

1 tablespoon pistachios

1 tablespoon raisins

1 tablespoon ghee (clarified butter)

Extra nuts and raisins for garnishing

Instructions

1. Set your sous vide machine to 185°F.

2. Soak the nuts and raisins in water for 30 minutes or until the raisins are plump.

3. Place the carrots, raisins, pistachios, almonds and into a large ziplock bag or a vacuum-seal bag. Remove all the air with the water displacement method or a vacuum-sealer. Seal and submerge the bag in the water bath and cook for 2 hours.

4. Meanwhile heat a saucepan over low heat. Add milk and simmer for an hour. Add sugar and stir until the sugar has dissolved.

5. When the carrots are ready, remove the carrots from the bath and bag and transfer it into the saucepan with the milk. Cook for about 5 minutes. Add cardamom powder and continue to cook while continuously stirring.

6. To serve, garnish with extra nuts and raisins. Serve at either hot or room temperature.

Light Raspberry Mousse

Ingredients

1 pound raspberries

¼ cup ultrafine sugar

3 tablespoons freshly squeezed lemon juice

½ teaspoon kosher salt

¼ teaspoon ground cinnamon

1 cup heavy cream

1 teaspoon vanilla extract

Instructions

1. Set your sous vide machine to 180°F.

2. Place the raspberries, sugar, lemon juice, salt, and cinnamon into a large ziplock or vacuum-seal bag. Seal the bag using the water displacement method or a vacuum-sealer and submerge in the water bath. Set the timer for 45 minutes.

3. When ready, remove the bag from the water bath and carefully pour the contents into a blender.

Pulse a few times before blending; puree the mixture until smooth. Set aside to cool to room temperature.

4. In a large mixing bowl, whisk the cream and vanilla until stiff peaks form. Gently fold in raspberry puree until fully incorporated and there are no white streaks.

5. Divide the mousse between 8 serving bowls and chill before serving.

Rich Pecan Pies

Serves 4

Ingredients

2 cups whole pecans, toasted and roughly chopped

1 cup maple syrup

1 cup light brown sugar

½ cup heavy cream

1 tablespoon molasses

4 tablespoons unsalted butter

½ teaspoon salt

6 large egg yolks

Freshly whipped cream, for serving

Instructions

1. Set your sous vide machine to 195°F and then grease your glass jars with butter or cooking spray.

2. Heat oven to 350°F

3. In a medium saucepan combine the maple syrup, sugar, cream, and molasses and place over medium heat Cook stirring occasionally until the sugar melts and the mixture has thickened slightly.

4. Remove the sauce from the heat and let it cool for 5 minutes at room temperature. Whisk in the butter and salt until the butter is melted and the sauce is glossy. Next whisk in egg yolks until smooth and the stir in the pecans.

5. Divide the filling between the prepared jars. Seal the jar tightly but leave enough space enough for air to escape.

6. Place jars in the prepared water bath and cook for 2 hours.

7. When done, remove the jars from the water bath and let the jars on a cooling rack. Serve with a dollop of whipped cream.

Sweet Corn Gelato

Serves 6

Ingredients

4 ears fresh corn, shucked

3 cups whole milk

1 cups heavy cream

1 cup granulated sugar

1 teaspoon kosher salt

6 large egg yolks

¼ cup crème fraiche

Instructions

1. Set your sous vide machine to 180°F.

2. Slice the kernels off the corncobs and place in a large saucepan with the milk, cream, salt, and sugar. Bring to ingredients to a simmer, then remove from the heat, and let the ingredients steep for 30 minutes.

3. Strain and discard the corn and cobs. Tip the corn-infused milk into a blender puree and the corn-infused milk and egg until smooth and frothy.

4. Pour the corn and egg mixture into a ziplock or vacuum-seal bag and remove all the air by using the water displacement method or a vacuum-sealer. Place into the hot water bath and cook for 30 minutes, make sure to shake the bag several times throughout the cooking process.

5. When ready, remove the bag from the hot water and chill in an ice bath.

6. When cold, pour the contents into a large bowl and whisk in the crèmefraiche. Continue to churn the mixture in an ice cream maker until set. Scoop the ice-cream into a large container and freeze until ready to serve.

Salted Caramel Ice Cream

Serves 6

Ingredients

1 ½ cups sugar

1 ¾ cups heavy cream

1 teaspoon sea salt

1 cup whole milk

5 egg yolks

1 teaspoon vanilla bean paste

Pinch of kosher salt

Instructions

1. Set your sous vide machine to 180°F.

2. In a large non-stick pan, heat one cup of the sugar, stirring frequently until it begins to melt. Then, swirl pan occasionally until sugar melts and caramelizes to a dark brown color.

3. Quickly, and carefully, whisk in one cup of the cream and continue to cook, stirring often. Stir until mixture is smooth and then stir in sea salt. Cool to room temperature.

4. In a blender, puree the egg, vanilla, and remaining cream, sugar, and milk until smooth and frothy.

5. Pour the mixture in a ziplock or vacuum-seal bag and cook in the water bath for 30 minutes. Make sure to shake the bag several times throughout the cooking process.

6. When ready, stir the caramel into the bag and chill overnight.

7. The next morning, churn the mixture in an ice cream maker until set. Freeze until ready to serve.

Rum Poached Peaches

Serves 4

Ingredients

4 peaches, peeled and halved, pit removed

½ cup dark rum

¼ cup sugar, plus ½ cup for syrup

Juice of ½ lemon

½ vanilla bean

3 whole cloves

¼ cup heavy cream

¼ cup plain yogurt

½ teaspoon vanilla

1 tablespoon honey

¼ cup sliced almonds, toasted

Instructions

1. Set your sous vide machine to 165.2°F.

2. While water heats, seal peaches, rum, ¼ cup sugar, lemon juice, vanilla bean and cloves into ziplock or vacuum-seal bag. Remove as much air as possible with the water displacement method or a vacuum-sealer. Cook in a hot water bath for 1 hour.

3. When peaches is done cooking, remove bag from hot water, and immediately chill in an ice bath.

4. Pour all poaching liquid from bag into saucepan and bring to boil over medium-high heat. Reduce heat to medium and then stir in remaining 1/2 cup sugar. Boil and reduce until thick and syrupy.

5. Whip the cream with sour cream with vanilla and honey until stiff peaks.

6. To serve, place 2 peach halves into bowl and drizzle the syrup on top. Spoon a dollop of cream on top and sprinkle with toasted almonds. Serve immediately.

Vanilla & Citrus Brioche Bread Pudding

Serves 4

Ingredients

1 cup whole milk

1 cup heavy cream

½ cup granulated sugar

¼ cup maple syrup

1 large egg, plus 2 large egg yolks

2 tablespoons orange juice

1 tablespoon orange zest

1 teaspoon vanilla bean paste

½ teaspoon kosher salt

4 cups brioche, cut into 1-inch cubes

Instructions

1. Set your sous vide machine to 170°F.

2. In a large mixing bowl, whisk together the milk, cream, sugar, maple syrup, orange juice, orange zest, vanilla paste, and salt. Add the brioche and gently toss. Make sure that the all bread pieces are coated with the egg mixture. Set aside for 5 minutes to soak.

3. Divide the bread mixture between 4 individual sealable glass jars. Seal loosely to allow steam to escape during the cooking process.

4. Place the jars into the prepared water bath and cook for 2 hours.

5. When ready, remove the jars from the water bath. Remove the lids and place the jars onto an oven safe baking sheet and broil until the tops of the pudding is golden brown.

6. Serve warm with a scoop of vanilla ice cream.

Vanilla Bean Pots de Crème

Serves 6

Ingredients

8 large egg yolks

½ cup granulated sugar

1 teaspoon vanilla bean paste or 1 whole vanilla bean, split lengthwise

Pinch kosher salt

1 cup heavy cream

½ cup whole milk

Instructions

1. Set your sous vide machine to 180°F.

2. In a blender, add the egg yolks, sugar, vanilla paste, and salt, and puree until smooth. Transfer mixture into a large bowl.

3. In a small saucepan, add the cream and milk. Bring to a simmer and then remove from the heat. You want the milk and cream to be just warmed through.

4. Slowly whisk the warm milk into the egg. Set aside to cool.

5. Divide the mixture between 6 individual sealable glass jars. Seal loosely to allow steam to escape and then place the jars into the hot water bath. Cook for 45 minutes.

6. When ready, remove the jars and let the jars cool at room temperature for about 10 minutes. Then transfer to an ice bath to chill.

7. Refrigerate for at least 4 hours before serving, or up to 1 week. Serve with your favorite fruit compote or as is.

Vanilla Frozen Yogurt

Serves 8

Ingredients

1 quart whole milk

3 tablespoons yogurt with live active cultures

½ cup honey

¼ cup granulated sugar

1 teaspoon vanilla bean paste

Instructions

1. Set your sous vide machine to 115°F.

2. In a medium saucepan over medium heat, heat the milk to 180°F and then pour the milk into a large canning jar. Let the milk cool until it reaches 100-120°F.

3. Stir in the yogurt and seal the jar with the lid. Place the jar in the water bath and set the timer for 24 hours. Cover the water bath with plastic wrap to minimize water evaporation. You may need to continuously top off the bath with more water to keep the jar submerged. Add water intermittently to keep the jar submerged.

4. When ready, remove the jar from the water bath and transfer to an ice bath. Let the yogurt completely cool before transferring it to a bowl. Whisk in the honey, sugar, and vanilla paste.

5. Tip the contents into an ice cream machine and churn until frozen and smooth.

6. Store in the freezer until ready to serve.

Double Chocolate Cheesecakes

Servings 4

Ingredients

12 oz. cream cheese softened to room temperature

2 oz. sour cream

2 eggs

1 teaspoon vanilla

3.5 oz. white chocolate

3.5 oz. milk chocolate

Extra white and milk chocolate chips to serve

Instructions

1. Set your sous vide machine to 176°F.

2. In a medium mixing bowl, beat together the cream cheese, sour cream, eggs and vanilla until smooth and creamy.

3. Melt the white chocolate in a microwave safe bowl in 30-second intervals in the microwave. Stir between each interval. Repeat the process with the milk chocolate

4. Portion the cream cheese mixture into two bowls. Stir in the melted white chocolate in one until completely mixed. Repeat with the milk chocolate and the second bowl of the cream cheese mixture.

5. Prepare your mason jars by lightly spraying it with some cooking spray. Portion out the white chocolate mixture into the jars.

6. Top each with a layer of milk chocolate cheesecake and then use a thin knife or a bamboo skewer to swirl the two batters together until it creates a marbled pattern.

7. Cover the jars tightly and gently place the jars into the prepared water bath. Cook for 2 hours or until just set.

8. When ready, remove the jars from the water and immediately sprinkle in the

Remaining white and milk chocolate ships. Replace the lids and let the residual heat melt the chocolate. Let the jars cool to room temperature and then chill overnight in the refrigerator.

9. To serve, serve the cheesecakes in the jars or run a sharp knife along the edge and then invert onto a dessert place.

Rhubarb Fool

Serves 4

Ingredients

2 cups diced rhubarb

½ cup light brown sugar

1 teaspoon vanilla bean paste

1 teaspoon cinnamon

Pinch kosher salt

1 ½ cups heavy cream

½ cup toasted almonds, chopped

Instructions

1. Set your sous vide machine to 180°F.

2. Place the rhubarb, sugar, vanilla paste, cinnamon, and salt into a large ziplock or vacuum-seal bag. Seal the bag with the water displacement method or a vacuum-sealer and then submerge into the hot water bath. Set a timer for 1 hour.

3. When ready, transfer the contents into a food processor and pulse until it becomes a chunky puree. Let the rhubarb puree cool to room temperature.

4. In another mixing bowl, whisk the heavy cream until it forms soft peaks, and then fold in the cooled rhubarb mixture.

5. Divide the mixture into 4 serving glasses and top with almonds. Serve immediately.

Conclusion

The recipes in this book are only an indication of the things you able to cook using your sous vide machine. As you continue to develop your skills and comfort with the method, you can start to apply the things you've learned to your own creations. Try thinking of a dish you love, and how you might be able to make a sous vide adaptation.

Always keep in mind that while recipes are highly specific, they are only designed this way to get the most out of the ingredients you cook. Once you've gotten comfortable with this element, cooking sous vide should begin to feel no different to using a seamer or a fry-pan. Over time, you'll start memorising the temperatures and cooking times of your favourite ingredients, and reaping the rewards of precision cooking.

As you continue to delight your family, friends, or even just yourself with tender meat and flavorsome vegetables, try experimenting more with your sous vide repertoire. There is a whole community of chefs like yourself transforming their kitchens into tiny restaurants who will be happy to share their experiences with you. As you continue to learn, you might even find that you have advice of your own to share!

Made in the USA
San Bernardino, CA
17 April 2018